THE
DAY
WE
HAD
CANDY
FLOSS

THE *DAY* WE *HAD* CANDY *FLOSS*

Catherine Lock

First published in 2025 by Catherine Lock,
in partnership with Whitefox Publishing

www.wearewhitefox.com

Copyright © Catherine Lock, 2025

ISBN 978-1-916797-16-1
Also available as an eBook
ISBN 978-1-916797-17-8

Catherine Lock asserts the moral right to be
identified as the author of this work.

All rights reserved. No part of this publication may be reproduced,
stored in a retrieval system or transmitted in any form or by any
means, electronic, mechanical, photocopying, recording or
otherwise, without prior written permission of the author.

Content warning: This book contains depictions of abuse,
sexual assault and suicide references. Reader discretion is advised.

This book is a work of fiction inspired by real events. While some
elements are based on personal memories and experiences, the
identifying features of people and places have been changed to
protect privacy. Descriptions of certain individuals and situations have
been altered or combined for the same purpose. Any similarities to
actual persons, living or dead, or real events are purely coincidental.

'So, we beat on, boats against the current...' is drawn from
The Great Gatsby by F. Scott Fitzgerald, first published in 1925,
and is currently in the public domain in the United States.
No permissions are required for use.

While every effort has been made to trace the owners of copyright
material reproduced herein, the author would like to apologise
for any omissions and will be pleased to incorporate missing
acknowledgements in any future editions.

Edited by Kay Coleman
Designed and typeset by seagulls.net
Cover design by Heike Schüssler
Project management by Whitefox Publishing

To my inspiration,
Sean and Mandy

Blood is the bond that ties,
and our journey of love goes on.

1

WISTFUL MUSINGS

Landry's Lair, Barston village
Friday 18 June 2023, 3 p.m.

Roisin is alone and will remain so until around five o'clock on Monday afternoon, and Roisin rarely walks into a quiet house void of men. The customary state of play being the inescapable sound of clickety-clack from busy fingers on keyboards, and notable business tête-à-têtes, interlaced with laughter and playful repartee. All of which reverberate throughout the expansive living space and galleried landing, telling of the day's deliberations. It is quite normal for Roisin to return home after a hunting and gathering event, laden with a supermarket haul, and have to negotiate the lurking presence of unfamiliar suits, well-polished shoes and spent coffee cups cluttering the office and kitchen, while attempting to appear intellectually with it, as she stuffs a cauliflower into the fridge, and muses regretfully, 'I do wish I had topped up my Dior Addict 976 lipstick, and checked for matte blue eyeliner smudge, before exiting the Jag.'

Today is different; it is a hazy Friday afternoon; the time is three o'clock and Roisin is relieved that her husband has left their home for a long weekend away with friends. The house is pristine, a picture-perfect abode, a scene worthy of an *ELLE Decoration* front page. Roisin has hungered for the solitude of the seventy-four hours that lie before her. No rhythm to follow, or pace to pick up, no clock to watch, no breakfast, lunch or dinner to serve. Just splendid restorative me-ism and self-indulgence, and gorging as and when she feels inclined. A welcome, slow-down interlude from the jammed-up calendar, the booked, paid-for and impossible-to-cancel schedule. A pause from the habitual hurtling chariot, fast-tracking to every exquisite taste, luxurious destination and pleasure a mere mortal can cram into their bucket list, and her husband's gold can buy.

With her mind craving to be empty, her heart searching for a lulling cadence, the torrent within her must still, leaving her free to think and act rationally, without impulse and without anger. A wrong move, a wrong decision, and her life, and what she has become, could change forever. Her day began with an early-morning trip to James's favourite deli to purchase a few of the finer tastes and delights that he enjoys. She still felt the need to perform and compose a convivial send-off, with all his favoured platters, for fear the last few moments he spent with her, before leaving the house for the weekend, would be viewed as underwhelming, a let-down. He notices everything and then, sometimes, nothing at all.

Roisin, sitting comfortably in her car, waits patiently for the parting of the automated iron gates, as she does each time she returns home. She consumes the image that lies before her as if sitting alone on a bench in an art gallery, completely focused. She observes every moving, flowing part, the extraordinary rays of sunlight and shadows jumping and darting between the long, reaching arms of the old oak trees as they appear to caress each other in the afternoon summer breeze. She unwinds her window and breathes in the floral scents as they dance across the wild wooded garden, as if instructed to do so by the hand of nature's conductor. At the centre of her view sits an imposing bespoke house, nestled in sculptured gardens.

Roisin is living her best millionaire's life. She massages the heated leather steering wheel like a purring cat kneading fervently with her claws, feeling special, feeling powerful. She knows she has arrived. Extending both her forearms, tightening her grasp, raising her shoulders, Roisin sits proudly pouting in the driver's seat.

'Hell, I deserve this life!' she blurts out defiantly. With no one else to hear the self-assuring declaration, she hopes the words and their meaning will swell through her blood, giving life to confidence and vanity. With a deepening inhalation, she is energised by excitable anticipation.

A vision of thundering muscled majesty, salivating teeth and tongues charge excitedly towards Roisin and escort her car next to the porch entrance. Jax and Coco, both black and tan Dobermanns, to some, represent the Devil's guardian, the vicious dog guarding a gangster's plunder. To their mistress, they epitomise unconditional loyalty, mellifluous evening snuggles and playful tumbles. Both successfully masquerade as persuasive strategic aggressors and are therefore fully worthy of her tenderness and parading.

For Roisin, returning home always brings with it an air of entitlement, a state of mind that she feels sits well with the house she owns, and the forever-giving, highbrow lifestyle, with its seemingly limitless price tag. Though what frequently ensues thereafter is a sense of foreboding fragility, of overwhelming loss and coal-black, smothering grief. Peering in the rear-view mirror to check the location of the dogs, she catches a glimpse of the imposter staring right back at her, her striking green eyes expressing only fear and doubt, her real self, the undeserving, the shackled.

As she turns off the ignition, she catches sight of James's bike, and his cycling gear, parked in front of the garage door. Roisin tentatively exits the car and gathers her shopping from the boot, wondering if James is watching her from the kitchen window. She opens the double porch door and notices he has brought down the suitcase she had packed for him the evening before. She immediately logs a note to self: must quiz James regarding any items he may have forgotten. Packing is not his forte. Roisin welcomes the wall of ice-cold air conditioning blasting her face and neck, rescinding the menopausal swelter. She steps towards the gold-rimmed oval mirror in the entrance hall, verifying if she looks the way she feels. Her eyes look tired and puffy, her morning makeup is smudged with perspiration and her usually tamed dark red hair has gone rogue with frizzy curls and wisps.

Kicking off her summer wedges, her broiling, blistering feet stand bare, relieved to sop up the healing coolness of the marble hallway floor, which is laid about the central sweeping resplendent oak and iron staircase.

'Well done, darling,' James remarks in a chipper manner, while skipping down the stairs, and after spotting the logo for the White Truffle Deli on the carrier bags huddled together on the hallway floor, 'Can we have lunch promptly at twelve-thirty? Roland, Humphrey and Leo are arriving at two. You know how Roland gets peeved at a sniff of dilly-dally.'

. . .

After sharing a selection of French cheeses, an exception being a Norwegian blue Nidelven Blå, and Jamon Iberico de Bellota 100%, accompanied with artisan breads and various condiments, ceremoniously washed down with a complementary 'one for the road' Amarone della Valpolicella Italian red, James plants a hasty token peck on Roisin's already poised lips, prompting her attention towards a 'to do' list.

'One job, darling,' he begins to spout, wagging his finger and tapping her nose. 'Remember, proper preparation prevents piss poor performance. Please do try and complete before my return.' His patronising, ritualistic dictum, one she knows well, and mostly said for humorous effect, comes with a 'I am in charge here, darling; remember who's the big boss; don't let the standards drop; consequences upon consequences'. Roisin always tends to err on the side of 'It's all a laugh', at the point of delivery, preferring to keep it light-hearted, and not piss on his fire, but the remark sure sticks in her throat, and keeps popping into her head, snapping her in the direction of 'must do better', which she knows, of course, is James's true intention.

Roisin peers discretely from afar, watching James as he hugs Roland with gusto and comedic bluster. She thinks he looks so much younger than his years when wearing his dark blue jeans and a casual shirt. Once the kerfuffle on the drive of loading bikes and luggage quietens down, without a parting glance, James slams shut the front door and proceeds to squeeze himself into the blacked-out Range Rover – a vehicle already crammed with jovial man-children presuming to misbehave for three nights and three days, post shedding their everyday paternal and significant-other steadfast fetters, starting from the moment they each clamber into their getaway vehicle.

Standing in the kitchen, with the gate control in her hand, Roisin watches the back end of the vehicle swing to the left at speed and out of view. For a moment, she holds her position and pauses, remembering, and longing for the days when the priority for both herself and James was a last-minute, ardent farewell bonk. Then she was always left standing at the front door glowing, waving off her beloved, missing him before he even reached the gate. Taking in his 'I love you' puppy dog gaze, still feeling the heat and throb between her legs and the tremble and fluster from rousing sex.

Destined for the Yorkshire Dales, James and friends will endeavour to track the sterling 'Tour de France, or Tour de Yorkshire' as it came to be referred in 2015.' The Lycra-clad, fully charged, testosterone-fuelled dad bod's benchmark for a successful trip will be a concoction of perpetual top-up beer stops, an unyielding barrage of borderline abusive bloke banter and unrelenting merciless character assassinations. Reaching the finish line is an achievement in itself – but arriving still as friends? That's nothing short of a miracle.

Roisin witheringly takes an uninterested glance over the aftermath of lunch. Suddenly feeling limp and lacklustre, she plunges herself into the head dining-room chair. Sensing a shrivelling away, she hunches her upper body forward, resting her elbows on the fourteen-seater, walnut dining-room table. Cupping her hands over her face, she closes her eyes. She needs a moment. After at least ten minutes of deep inhalation, and slow and complete exhalation through pursed lips, she feels calm and clear-headed enough to reach for the Valpolicella and finish off the last of it. Roisin detects hints of Dior Sauvage, James's most recent cologne, still lingering in the kitchen. She feels a rise of emotion swell from deep within, as a tear releases and meanders gently over her cheek and down her chin. She still loves James; he is in every corner of her world.

He is the only man to walk with her down the aisle, to declare his love and promise 'till death do us part'. As she takes in the quiet of the house, her thoughts drift back to the *Pretty Woman* moment. Roisin had known James for many years in a client–patient capacity, but their relationship took an unexpected turn and went beyond what it should. It was complicated. They were both on the same page, trying to run away from what had been before. Both not looking, but open to a low-input, high-octane, no-strings-attached liaison, preferably with a no-drama, easy-exit clause attached. After enjoying four weeks of intimacy, equating to four nights fucking, and four days of high-end entertainment in London, they each got the protocol: no conversation unleashing remorse, melancholic moodiness, exes and failures, and definitely no clingy tears. That's the rules.

No words of warning were necessary between them. They each knew these conversations were off limits, and would be a deal-breaker. The first four weeks of their togetherness were a riot of rejuvenation and finding oneself again through the other. Those four days and four nights were both refreshing and uncomplicated, until the *Pretty Woman* moment, that is. What he paid that day, revealed to her her worth and value. She had a game to play, and she now had a winning hand. The details of that day are still very clear in Roisin's mind. She recalls it being a Saturday, midday in late July, and James had alluded to a pre-planned surprise for Roisin, one he suggested they would both enjoy. The journey to London had gone very well and considering the passionate exhilaration of their previous four dates, her expectations were soaring.

She found herself in Harrods, Knightsbridge, London in the Michelin 3-star, Chef Masa, Sushi Bar, sharing a bottle of Veuve Clicquot with James, while choosing her first taste of sushi and sashimi. She had never eaten raw fish before, or any kind of Japanese food. She was both excited to try something so unusual for her, and to impress James, who so far, seemed to have the gift of the Midas touch. Maybe he will surprise me with something gold and expensive, she wondered during reciprocal flirtatious handling and lingering looks, intent on promising an evening of sexual adventure.

'Oh God! Blimey, James, raw tuna and soy sauce is just amazing! I am in shock. Kiss me, James,' she demanded, ready to take what she wanted.

'You're drunk, Roisin, and I should say, delightful with it,' James replied, being coy with his answer, before sucking down a raw sliver of salmon in a disturbingly suggestive manner.

'What can I say, James? I am a lush,' sloshing back the last sparkle from her champagne flute. 'That's all it takes. I am now in the realms of intense, multiple-sensory horniness. My clitoris is begging for you right now.'

James, never one to be crass in public, lowered his voice, moved in close, placed her hand on his groin, and whispered, 'I like my food first, and then I fuck.'

Roisin, digging her manicured nails into his hardened bulge, retorted with a tiger's growl. 'This bad boy has a job on, and a bitch waiting.'

James handed her a bowl of hot, salted edamame beans with a provoking 'You have to earn this bad boy, woman' grin on his face.

After a last wipe of the napkin, and a flip of his Panama hat, James grabbed Roisin by the hand, joggling her off her stool. 'Come on, my waiting bitch. Follow me.'

'The lipstick will have to wait,' she thought while being pulled hurriedly through huge departments, corridors and lifts, until James finally came to a stop in front of the ladies' lingerie counter. He tipped up the front of his Panama, leant over a little towards the stunning young woman with the most perfectly sensual, dark almond eyes and flawless makeup.

'This is Roisin, here for your styling service, with you, Zaliki, I think, looking at your name badge.' Her charms were not unnoticed by James as his attention seemed to linger over her shapely figure longer than was necessary.

'Oh God, what has he done?' Roisin questioned herself, cringing while firming up an appreciative smile.

'Please come this way, Roisin,' Zaliki purred, swinging her tightly dressed, hourglass figure from side to side very slowly. Roisin felt her stomach somersault. She was sure she heard James let out a, 'Mmm, fucking great arse,' as he shimmied alongside her for an uninterrupted panoramic view of pert, wriggling arse.

'Of course he did,' she thought. They arrived at a small room with a single-curtained cubicle, a few cream hooks on the wall, and a small chair tucked in the corner. Rather like a doctor's examination room, but beautifully decorated in plush wallpaper and with a swish purple velvet curtain and tassel tie-back.

Once inside the room, Zaliki opened the opposite door and turned to James. 'Mr Landry, this is where you can relax, enjoy a glass of champagne, and take in the delights on offer. And, considering you have an unlimited spend with us today, we may be here for some time.' She flashed her pearly whites, brighter still from glimmering with sincerity and the perfect sales pitch. 'And please feel free to order what you wish from our courtesy drinks menu,' she added, swishing away. Watching James settle into a comfortable chair, cross his legs, and start to read one of the newspapers from a pile on the small coffee table, Roisin sensed he was quite familiar with his surroundings. Taking out her tape measure, Zaliki proceeded in all her perfect ways to collate the lengths, the widths and the preferences of Roisin's look.

She then left the cubicle, armed with the purpose of revamping Roisin's entire wardrobe, up-styling and clothing her with designer labels and a gloss of glamour. Roisin, feeling slightly hijacked into this situation, had a few moments to mull over the detail and process this surprise. She wondered if she looked so poor and tatty that James felt embarrassed to show her off as his girlfriend, and without style to the point that she needed someone else to choose the clothes she wore. She grumbled to herself, staring at her twisted face in the mirror, feeling like the sparkle had been rubbed away from their date.

Roisin, flip-flopping between 'What a lucky girl I am, lap up the luxury', to licking her wounds, tried to find some middle ground in her reasoning. 'OK,' she ruminated, 'maybe my much-searched-for charity-shop finds are not so hot, and who wouldn't want to wear Christian Dior or Balenciaga, especially when you're not the one painfully paying for the privilege on your credit card six months later. And maybe all that champagne, still obscuring my thoughts, is making me too precious,' she concluded, just as Zaliki returned with her arms full of dazzling dresses and sensual lingerie.

After pawing at the beautiful materials, sumptuous designs and lacy garments, Roisin chose a Coco Chanel dress and a midnight-blue, silk Agent Provocateur ensemble to show off to James. Zaliki had honoured her worth. All the evening wear was elegant and thrilling. Roisin was left trembling, as she enjoyed the feel and quality of silk and the touches of lace, as the lingerie slipped over the curves of her bottom and breasts. Roisin turned her head back, looking over her right shoulder at the mirror behind her, admiring how her ivory skin contrasted beautifully with the midnight blue. 'Oh my God,' she whispered to herself, biting her lower lip, 'now I will impress James.'

After slipping on a pair of high heels, she coated her lips liberally with her more vibrant evening lipstick, and made lively her hair, with a throw forward of her head, a ruffle with her fingers, and then finished off with a flick and twizzle of her fringe, framing her new confident and forward-thinking self. With the stride and pose of a catwalk model, Roisin pushed open the door, strutted a little, and placed her hand on her hip, adopting the 'needing a pee pose'. James, a little taken aback by the drama of her entrance and the sight before him, widened his eyes, and his grin.

'Delicious, darling. That's a goer,' he stated slowly, in a deep and husky voice, giving the thumbs up. Roisin, feeling rather brash, took ownership of his half-full champagne flute.

'I knew there was something missing,' she announced assuredly. Over the next two hours, what ensued was: clothes on, clothes off, thumbs up, thumbs down, a lot of champagne, quite a few Hendrick's and tonic, a lot of sexual teasing and tension, strategic flashes of underwear, and a definite shift in the balance of power.

By the end of the show, James demanded they leave with her wearing Safiyya, the onyx evening dress, and whatever it was he managed to catch a glimpse of when she wrapped her leg around the door and pretended to fuck. Dressed to kill, she straddled James as he sat on the husband chair. He grabbed her hips, forcing her back and forth over his hard-on.

'I need you right now,' he grunted and growled, pawing at the hem of her not-yet-paid-for dress, raising it higher up her thighs, exposing the midnight blue veiling her sweet spot.

'You pay the bill and then I fuck,' she ordered. 'Payback,' she quipped, before pulling his bottom lip away sharply with her teeth.

James came away many thousands of pounds lighter, and Roisin knew she had at least one night ahead to enjoy her dominance. It was a quick dash out into the cold night air. James soon hailed a black cab, his grasping becoming more urgent, his need to ravage unstoppable. That night, in the opulent bedroom of the Langham Hotel, while savouring the expensive feel of her silk midnight-blue lingerie against her clitoris, she decided she was going to take full control of James. She demanded he lie back on the bed, with both hands gripping the metal bars in the headboard. It was his night to be submissive and to be pleasured at her will.

At this point it was all very much an exciting transaction. He gave her a bite of luxury, a rush of power, and she could still feel its unique taste in her mouth and in her loins. 'The only movement I want to see is your tongue rolling from side to side, and your cock standing to attention,' she commanded strongly, while squeezing his facial cheeks together firmly with her hand and straddling his torso. James, conceding without resistance to her requests, was delighted with being massaged, kissed, licked, sucked and fucked beyond his own satisfactions and to the point of falling asleep.

'Thank you, my Celtic crush ... I have still left you waiting and wanting, Roisin,' he mumbled through his tiredness.

'You paid for it, darling,' she replied as she reached for her Duracell mate: he needed no instruction. With swift handling, she played her friend and came to a place of ecstasy. With her jaw clenched and her body writhing, she took every vibration into her places of pleasure, trying to muffle her sheer delight. James woke up at the sound of her groans as she went for a second time. He pulled the covers over his head.

'Go to sleep, you fucking horny bitch,' he demanded, desperate for sleep.

The *Pretty Woman* moment transformed their casual fling into a relationship, one of need and respect for each other. They both began to let go of the toughened exterior, keeping silent their anguish and the hurt still gouging away at their emotions, blockading their authentic selves, and preventing a place where love might flourish. They both shared the same wounds and needed the same drug. The sex became familiar and fun, their thoughts of care and kindness, and their hearts filled with longing and love, both harbouring a simmering sense they had something worth keeping.

. . .

With a harsh sense of realisation, Roisin snaps out of her daydreaming. 'What point is there reliving the pearls of the past, trying to rebuff the present,' she thinks, annoyed with herself. The reality of the here and now hits her hard. She feels the need to find an answer, make sense of the sparring going on in her head and stop the searing pain agonising through her heart and mind. James had visited Roland Reeves, one of his oldest friends, and financial adviser, in London two weeks prior to their cycling trip. He informed Roisin of this last-minute arrangement, suggesting critical timing was of the essence and crucial to business planning.

He had frequented the same hotel on several occasions over the previous year. 'Drinking and socialising too,' James would say, 'was integral and at the core of strategic decision-making.' 'Loosen their ego, close the contract' was a phrase Roisin often heard her husband parrot from his office at home.

She never had the worry, or reason to bring into question the possibility, of infidelity. James had always been so reassuring of his love and loyalty for her, even more so when he spent time away. When he returned home, he would often reveal the escapades of business associates, particularly Roland, whom she was told had an open marriage with his naturally beautiful and willowy Korean wife. He never once suggested it was a lifestyle that he envied or wanted for himself. Both James and Roisin had a lot of relationship experience behind them, they both endorsed monogamy from day one, and reaffirmed that decision on their wedding day. So, the moment it came to light that his visits to London in mid-April were about a different kind of business: an abandonment of his wedding vows, with nights spent with Ulyana, Mariya and Vanka – Russian escort girls – her world caved in before her very eyes.

His mistake was not knowing that his phone was linked to his new iPad, the one he left at home. His messages and diary entries revealed the dates and times and the crude comments he had shared with Roland about the girls, leading up to and after his lurid encounters. Roisin saw his location in real time, which girl he invited to his hotel, and the date he had planned for her next visit under the name Milaya Investments. He even received a photo of each girl in various stages of undress, for him to agree on, or pass on to the next option.

Roisin still feels the gut-wrenching tightening in her stomach and tastes the stench of the diarrhoea erupting from her bowels throughout the days and nights he was away. The stress and heartache were disabling. She worked through the nightmare and by the time James walked through the door with words of love rolling easily off his tongue, she presented herself as the loving and giving wife he had come to expect. It was not hard to hide her tears and sadness. She is still very much consumed with grief and guilt after Noah's death ten months ago.

What they had before Noah, his youngest son, took his own life, has splintered into a thousand wounding shards, indifference and self-preservation. Their demise has been slow and painful, and, for Roisin, reminiscent of her past failures and breakups with Andreas and Ian. The overwhelming feeling of helplessness and loss, she fears, has caught up with her once again. She needs space and time to work out an exit plan.

2

BETWEEN THE LAYERS

Friday, 3 p.m.

Roisin feels compelled to venture back into her past, to revisit the morbid, the bleak and the reasons why she made the choices she did, her darkest and her brightest of times, believing somehow reminiscence, clarification and re-capturing will help her deal with the present, and help her save what she has. Holding a comforting hot chocolate drink and with Jax and Coco lying over her legs and stomach, requesting her attention, she soon begins to relax on the floppy settee in the sunroom. Roisin begins to fall into the chambers of her past, her mind sizzling like sherbet lemon on a raw and sensitive tongue. She starts to mull things over. 'Where do I begin? What is important, of value? What can I learn from stuff that happened years ago, or decisions I made? ... What is the point of it? Just go to sleep,' she demands of herself, but she knows sleep will only put off the inevitable.

She leaves the comfort of the sunroom and heads to the garage. With some effort, Roisin drags an old, scuffed leather brown case through the house, up the stairs and onto her bed. A familiar case: one she had placed in the garage twelve years ago on the back of the shelf, and at the back of her mind, on the day she moved in with James. It was a day of new beginnings, of joy and happiness; there was no place for the doom and gloom of her past.

That case represents what came before, a time she prefers to forget. With clenched teeth, and a forceful heave, she prises open the once-pleasing brass clasps, now tarnished with rust. Inside, photos of all descriptions sit piled high, some with their corners creased, trapped and misshapen by the outer edges of the case. Layers and layers of snippets in black and white, wrinkled and stained, bright and colourful, smooth and shiny; all revealing bits of faces, smiles and playful places; whole lives portrayed and entombed as one performance, in one theatre. Roisin tips the open case onto her bed, tumbling the photos in every direction. She picks at a few sticking to the inner surfaces of the case, careful not to inflict further damage.

'Where do I start?' she mumbles to herself, hands splayed out over her temples, staring at what lies before her, awaiting an answer. She decides to head to the fridge. A sizeable chocolate bar and a cuppa always give clarity to any dilemma, an essential contrivance for enabling the functioning normalities of family life, she finds. Like any 'strategic professional' housekeeper, squirreling your treats away out of sight is a requisite. Two wine cooler sleeves in the fridge, bulging with choccy bars is the one constant in her day. She heads back upstairs to her bedroom. The photos, thrown together haphazardly, rejected and stuffed in the case in no chronological order, seem insignificant.

After a long, deep sigh, clarity prevails. Roisin stands over her bed looking at the photos waiting to be sorted, scrutinised and discarded. She knows this road will bring an avalanche of thought and deliberation. Memories upon memories, some joyous, many provoking, a few with hurt and angst. 'Is it worth the grief, regurgitating all the past?' she ponders. She draws in a deep breath, closes her eyes and shuffles her hand between the layers in the pile, singling out one photo.

. . .

'And so, we beat upon our breast against the here and now, lurching back ceaselessly into the past, the unfinished, the regretful, the longed for; lacerating old wounds for little reward … better to battle for a clear day than fumble in the dark.'

3

LOOK UPON WITH IRISH EYES

Andersonstown, Belfast, November 1967

It's Friday 4 p.m. and Roisin, poised, stares with interest at the black-and-white photo in her hand. Scribbled on the back are the names: Niall, Roisin, Darra; the address: 22 Falls Road; and the date: November 1967. She turns over the photo, intrigued at the image of her brother Darra as a toddler, and her three-year-old self. Darra is sitting perched on Niall's knee and he is looking down at the floor. His cheeks appear rounded and full, his nose snotty and wet. Darra looks grumpy and uninterested in Niall, whose hand appears to support his posture, or in his sister Roisin, whose right arm lies flung over Niall's shoulder. Her eyes are laughing and looking up at him. Her red curls sit at the nape of her pearly white neck, and her body is held nurturingly against his chest. Smiling, Niall appears to be transfixed by the little girl's adoration of him. She looks happy, enjoying his attention.

Roisin wonders what she would have been thinking as a child in that moment ... maybe 'You must be my daddy now. This is how daddies look and smell.' His nicotine-stained hands and the musty smell emanating from his clothes and breath may have reminded her of her own father. Roisin looks at photos of when she lived with her Uncle Niall and Aunt Maeve as a young child, along with Darra and Orla, her younger sister. She feels no connection to her Uncle Niall and Aunt Maeve and was never interested in their story. She was forever disappointed that they never told her of the whereabouts of their father over this period, or what happened to their mother. All she got to know was that her own father lived with Uncle Niall most of his childhood and she never got to experience the joy and wisdom that grandparents may have brought to her life. She later learnt from her own father that he preferred to keep his secrets, tell lies and shift culpability on to their absent mother, unconcerned that his actions would leave a lifetime of bitterness and reeling rejection for Roisin, her brother and her sister.

Roisin later returned to the house in Falls Road with her father in 1977, aged thirteen, and again in 1981, at seventeen years old. She found the threadbare, dirty carpets and smoked-stained 1950s-style, peeling wallpaper unchanged and repelling. There was no truth to be found, only more lies, and war on the streets. As the older child, Roisin was more discerning and better at handling her father's moods and demands, so he always approached her to pass instructions on to her brother and sister. She felt useful and important and, in a strange way, closer to him, even though the communications were harsh and matter of fact and without a touch, or a warm smile to ease her worry.

Often, he was busy, but mostly she remembers him sitting for the longest time in his chair, appearing frozen, focused on the TV, with his legs raised on the pouffe and his denim jeans rolled up to his knees. His paw-like hairy hands placed on his thighs, or dipping unremittingly into a Quality Street tin. He never offered her a chocolate, even when he caught her peeking in the tin. She would stand and stare at the side of his face, wanting to speak, but afraid of an angry backlash. She thought his large head looked square and his long, wiry, ginger beard resembled the scrubbing brush that sat on the kitchen sink by the taps, and that the moment she annoyed him, it would turn into a fierce wild animal and eat her. She often found it strange that, despite his unusually large ears, he never seemed to hear her or her brother and sister crying. He never came closer to them, even when they stood nearby, sniffling and hungry for food.

Roisin and her siblings' first trip to Belfast with their father on the overnight ferry from Liverpool turned out to be an exciting adventure and could not have been further from the daily rot of home life. Roisin thought her father to be kinder, brighter and more approachable than he usually was, and during the many hours they all sat and lay down together in their shared bunk bed cabin, their father, like a red fox caring for its cubs, snuggled next to them in bed and protected them. Roisin remembers how they were so used to being subdued at home and that this feeling of being relaxed with their father on the ferry was something new. They were not sure how to respond to him at first, but she remembers wanting to sit close to him and touch him.

Once on dry land and leaving Belfast Docks, Roisin found the presence of prowling British armed soldiers and the ten-foot red metal barricades at every main entrance into Belfast shocking, but the 'Summer of 69' political mural on Hopewell Crescent, just off the Crumlin Road, turned her fear into curiosity as to what was happening in her father's homeland. During the drive to 22 Falls Road, there were so many disturbing sights that caught Roisin's attention: the huge metal gates, railings and partitioning walls on Cupar Way, separating the warring factions, that seemed to go on forever.

She stared at the individual murals from the back seat of the black cab, the colourful works of graffiti art depicting violent events, and the turmoil of lives lived, shouting of political allegiances. She tried to catch their message, before they quickly disappeared. She wondered how the painters managed to reach the top, near to the roof on a house, or on towering concrete walls. How did they draw the outlines of people on rough surfaces, and did they use extra-large brushes? Roisin asked so many questions en route, which became an annoyance to her father. The black cab driver, who had a few questions of his own, was able to gratify her interest with the lowdown on the reality of what he called 'life as a freedom fighter living in the war zone'.

Just after they turned into Conway Street, she saw the burning shell of what looked to be a lorry lying on its side. Rolling plumes of dark smoke bellowed up towards the sky. There was dirt and debris littered around, empty bottles, broken glass and bricks strewn over the kerbs; the destruction had been sectioned off with barbed wire fencing. Three soldiers were circling the scene, agitated and alert, watching and listening to a group of young men, not so far away, hurling bricks and abuse in their direction.

'Aye it's a shit show. Be glad ye did not arrive in the wee hours, now,' the driver said, matter of fact, looking at her father.

Darra and Orla spent most of the journey catching up on sleep, and both seemed reluctant to wake up from nuzzling into the comfort of the back seat of the car. Roisin's mind began to race, creating its own version of what lay ahead of them …

A bomb suddenly exploded very close to their car, killing all the people who were walking along the pavement. The woman wearing the pretty floral scarf over her head, pushing the big navy and cream pram with the large silver metal wheels, while her baby slept. The old man sitting on a doorstep smoking a pipe, wearing a black cap and an oversized coat with its collar up, keeping his ears warm. The children playing drop ball against the brick wall of the terrace house with the peeling brown paint and the dirty windows.

Everything a writhing mass of blood and guts. Grasping the front of her coat belt, Roisin recoiled, as she imagined the agony the people would feel as they took their last breath. She imagined the obliteration of street life, its normalcy, now bits on the ground and strewn over their car. Twisted bodies lay charred among the ashes. Someone was running away amid a frenzy of bullets, screaming as they hit the ground, bloodied, and dying in front of her.

'And what of ourselves?' she thought in a panic. 'Are we going to be beaten up, taken with our father, dragged away, only to be gassed? That's what happens in a war zone,' she inferred to herself. 'That is what's happening to Anne Frank and the children in the book I am reading, *The Diary of a young girl*.' Roisin looked over at her brother and sister sleeping, blissfully unaware of the chaos that was about to erupt.

She readied herself to forcibly wake them up and get them out of the car to run away from harm. Today, they had arrived safely at 22 Falls Road, but she wondered if tomorrow, or the next day, or the day after that would be the day when she needed to save Darra and Orla.

The black cab came to a stop, jolting her from her dark imaginings. Roisin watched her father's face light up with excitement as he looked towards the couple standing on their doorstep. Roisin had given no thought to the moment when she would meet Uncle Niall and Aunt Maeve again. Their greeting of long hugs and kisses while stood at the front door to their house, made her recoil with distaste.

'Oh my God, my boy,' Niall voiced with surprise, grabbing her father, Seamus by his coat, with tears in his eyes.

Aunt Maeve ruffled his hair. 'Git yourself in here, brother, so I can git hold of ye,' she said very quickly in a Northern Irish twang, one Roisin struggled to understand. She noticed her father's voice, too, had suddenly become more Irish when he spoke.

It was an easy first few days, seeing their father parade them around, being tactile and fatherly. Roisin had never seen him display such warmth; it brought a sense of relief to her troubled heart. Darra came out of his dark mood, and Orla began to giggle and run around the house, something she had never done before. Late into the evenings, resounding Irish voices would recite Republican military songs together with passion and a few whiskeys. Roisin recognised the tune of one of the songs, 'The Soldier's Song,' as one she had heard many times before, played by her father at home in Leicester on the record turntable.

It turned out be a strange week, with only two visits permitted outside of the house. A visit to the cathedral, where Aunt Maeve pushed down hard on the shoulders of all three children when they each reached the end of the pew where they would be sitting, making them bend down before the statues of Mary and Jesus Christ.

'Git ye down before our Mary, the mother of God; show some respect and reverence to the blessed sacrament; and draw the sign of the cross on ye chest,' she snapped in a high-pitched voice, looking sternly at the children, with a screwed-up face and a stand-offish folding of her arms.

Roisin thought her Aunt Maeve to be much scarier than the headmistress at her school. The children dared not disobey her commands. The children watched their father jump to attention at her every utterance. Her sharp tone and beady eyes were penetrating, and the children feared the punishment for not doing as they were told would be much worse than what they received at home.

'She must be a monster,' Darra whispered into Roisin's ear, while they were both kneeling on the red cushion behind the pew. Roisin batted him away with a panicky shush.

The second time they left the house, they visited Andersonstown Social Club with their father and Uncle Niall, who shook the hands of a group of men standing at the entrance door.

The three children were ushered down into the cellar by their father, where they were told to sit on beer barrels. He brought them fizzy drinks, crisps and a pack of dominoes to play with. 'You're English,' their father reminded them in a snappy tone while wagging his finger. 'Keep your voices down and don't leave the cellar. If you need to pee, go over there, right in that corner,' he said, cocking his head in the direction of the rat traps, and then running briskly up the stairs, disappearing out of sight. The children looked over at the corner where their father had indicated, turning to each other with faces filled with horror. They dared not move an inch, for surely the rats would be behind the boxes of crisps and nuts, and in the dusty dark corners, waiting to pounce and sink their chisel-like gnashers into their lily-white ankles.

They sat for hours in the cold, listening to the constant humming noise and voices coming from above, shivering and becoming more distressed. Orla sniffled quietly as she was ordered. Darra and Roisin squabbled mercilessly, thumping and kicking each other, over everything and nothing at all. Roisin, annoyed, grabbed a packet of crisps out of Darra's hands, and crushed them under her foot. Darra, out of desperation, in a hastened panic, peed in the corner, twice.

The children were not disappointed to be leaving the dark terrace house in Falls Road, the mean Aunt Maeve or the war zone. As she saw her father return to his normal aloof and short-tempered self, Roisin knew the moment they arrived home, they, too, would again be fighting in a war zone of their own.

. . .

It takes some time for Roisin to gather up the black-and-white photos from among all the others. There are not so many, and it would not have taken so long if she had not stopped to glance at each one so thoughtfully, taking in the faces and their expressions, wondering what they were thinking at that time, and how they made her feel. She spends some time lingering over the photo of her father as a young man, trying to find some connection with him, an understanding of his journey to see if her judgement of who he was to her was open to change.

She thinks he looks about sixteen, and he appears smart in his black suit, jumper, and white shirt with its large, winged collar, nearly reaching to the ends of his shoulders. She notices how the scene has been carefully staged outside in a garden, with his parents sitting on wooden chairs, dressed in what is probably their Sunday best. The nine young women, all lined up and standing behind her father and their parents, some fair and red-haired, some dark, all look pretty, slender and beautifully dressed in their 1940s dresses and pencil skirts. Roisin supposes her father, standing in the middle of his family, with the arms of his sisters draped over him, was most likely always the centre of attention.

Roisin remembers them all sitting together by a hot stove in Aunt Maeve's kitchen in 1977, listening as Maeve reminisced over her old photos and told the children their father's childhood story. Roisin remembers feeling bemused as to why he was so remote, when he had known the joy of being wanted and loved by so many. Aunt Maeve purposely omitted details and avoided answering any questions the children asked of her: why did they live with strangers when they were younger? What happened to their mother and where is she now? ... She would not even mention her name. 'Ya da is all ye need. Shut up now,' she said, screwing up her face, then playfully grasping their father's beard with her fingers.

Roisin and her siblings tried so hard over the years to show their father that they needed his love and guidance, and how much they wanted to love him in return, but there was no history, no bond between them. He was a stranger. It was not until after his death that Roisin and her siblings tried to piece together the puzzle of his life in an attempt to understand why he became the man he was, and hopefully find peace within themselves. Their father, Seamus Hugh Quinn, the last child of ten and longed-for male and heir, was born in Belfast in 1945 in the same terrace house on the Falls Road that was now owned by his older sister Maeve and her husband Niall Brennan.

He came into the world at a time when his forty-three-year-old mother Kathleen had believed her birthing days were over. A glowing mass of bright blond curly hair tumbling around his plump rosy face, piercing blue eyes and a birthday on the same day as Christ himself, gave promise to a prized childhood. He was revered, ruined even, by his Catholic family who deemed him heaven sent. As a young man, Seamus thought very little of political aspirations, rather being content to run amok unchecked, and free to enjoy being the reckless, forceful young man that he was. His life was, however, defined by IRA rebellion.

Roisin's Uncle Niall, short and stocky in stature, with a finger-styled, Brylcreemed teddy-boy quiff and facial features resembling a smiling, persuasive grizzly bear was very much the patriarchal mentor within the community. He held a position of standing within the IRA as a recruiter, although no one at the time was announcing such. It was a time of 'careless talk costs lives and retribution'. On a dark dank November evening in 1963, one month before Seamus turned eighteen, Maeve ushered her beleaguered brother onboard a ship bound for the English mainland. Seamus, a youth, scurried in the dead of night for protection, or for deadly intent, no one knew. Later, his offspring questioned 'the blank pages' of their father's life, wondering what secrets he had to hide.

. . .

Roisin thinks back to her relationship with her father. She has never really reflected on who he really was as a person. She could never get past her wounds as a youngster. She blames him for so much of the hurt she suffered, and for what her brother and sister went through. Looking at his family photos, she believes he had a family that adored him, he had choices, and he turned his back on those who needed him and wanted to love him. She recalls how at the age of seventeen, she was living in a filthy bedsit and she was desperate for him to help and care for her.

It was after midnight, 29 April 1981. She had rolled herself into a ball on the floor. Her back was against an old, soiled cream settee, her head pushed down between her knees, she was rocking back and forth, trying to cry away the loneliness and the despair that she was feeling. She had turned her back on her faith and friends from her place of worship and was feeling full of shame. She was sure everyone now despised her and this was her punishment for mistakes she had made. Roisin remembers how desperate and lost she was at that time, knowing she had no one to turn to for help.

She recalls the fear she felt, knowing she was in debt and awaiting eviction, and the relief when Darra and Orla visited her the next day, telling her that Dad wanted her to come to Ireland to visit Uncle Niall and Aunt Maeve. She recalls the sadness in their eyes staring back at her, waiting for an answer. Even now, Roisin knows she had no choice but to go to Belfast. It was her only way of escaping her misery. She secured a room in a homeless refuge for when she returned to Leicester and, on 3 May, Roisin found herself once again greeting Aunt Maeve and Uncle Niall at the door of 22 Falls Road. The war zone looked very much the same, but this time she felt numb and was uninterested in her surroundings.

The journey from England was uneventful. Her father offered only long, penetrating looks and said very little. The next day, Aunt Maeve took the children to communion, and forcibly placed a cross around Roisin's neck before leaving the car. 'Put this on, ye heathen, Mary, mother of God,' she said in an uncompromising manner. 'Ya da says you must stay here with me. Ye been walking with the Devil. Father O'Donnell will straighten ye out.' Roisin stayed silent, she felt her cheeks redden and tried to suppress the need to breathe faster. She had no fight left in her.

On 5 May, all hell broke loose. The Falls Road became a battle-ground. British soldiers and local people came head-to-head in the street, shouting, rioting and throwing rocks and petrol bombs. Gunshots dispersed the crowds on either side. Roisin, Darra and Orla hid upstairs in their bedroom, peering out just above the window ledge, curiosity getting the better of their fear. Red flashes and the deafening shrill of emergency vehicles charging past their window filled the night sky.

Suddenly, Aunt Maeve was shouting at the top of her voice. 'He's dead, he's dead. Bobby Sands is dead.' The voices downstairs became enraged, swearing and calling for retribution.

'We are English. Are we going to die, Roisin?' Darra whispered in a frightened, broken voice.

Roisin hesitated with her reply. 'Uncle Niall will save us,' she said, unconvinced this would be the case. Recalling what she had seen earlier on the bedroom wall, Roisin swiftly lifted her head above the bedcovers and stared at a photo of Bobby Sands and nine other men on a large poster headed 'British Prisoners of War, Hunger Strikers, don't let them die'.

On 7 May, thousands of people followed the funeral procession of Bobby Sands through Andersonstown and along the Falls Road. As she stood in the rain with her brother and sister on the doorstep of the house, they watched the mass of heaving crowds following the coffin draped with the tricolour Irish flag flanked by six masked IRA men carrying assault rifles and dressed in military uniforms, black berets and black gloves. Roisin, Darra and Orla stood side by side, gripped by the events playing out right in front of them.

'Can you see Father and Uncle Niall, Roisin?' Darra asked excitedly, stretching his neck and grinning from ear to ear.

'We need to go home now,' Roisin thought, 'before Darra becomes Uncle Niall's next project.'

. . .

It's five o'clock on Friday afternoon, but Roisin feels like James left the house many hours ago. She is sitting on her bed, continuing to flick through her old photos. The faces of her Irish uncles, aunts and cousins, the memory of the poster hanging on the bedroom wall of Bobby Sands and the hunger strikers, and the violence in the streets, now all faded and meaningless. All that is left is a sense of relief that the sliding doors of her time and that of her brother and sister, did not lead to a life in Belfast, living with Aunt Maeve and Uncle Niall. Despite Roisin returning to England with the knowledge that she was now homeless and her future uncertain, remaining in Ireland, or living with her father again, never once crossed her mind.

She is sure if Darra had stayed in Ireland, he would have thrown himself into a man's world of drinking, carrying a gun and maybe dying for the Irish cause. Orla, she thinks, may have fared better with the support of her Irish sisters and being a part of a close-knit community, and her father, too, may have had the support he needed from his family to raise his children. Maybe they would have all had the family life they craved and been content with who they were. However, Roisin suspects that had she stayed, she would have never come to know the luxuries or the wealth she now enjoys, or experienced the travels she has made across the globe.

4

OF ALL THE MEN

With a broad sweep of her arm, Roisin moves the photos from her side of the bed, piling them onto the side where James sleeps, making room to stretch out her legs. Roisin is sure of one thing: like her sister, she did not want to be with a man remotely like their father. They had come to know the consequences of harsh words, violence and a cold heart. Sadly though, ascertaining unfeigned love and trust was a skill Roisin did not come to possess until later in life. She plumps up her pillows and asks Google to play her playlist, something she would normally feel guilty about doing late in the afternoon, especially if James was working in his office. Sinking into her pillow, she drifts into her favourite sounds. With the soulful voice of Etta James singing 'At Last' taking over her thoughts, she tries to put aside the trauma in her marriage, longing to return to and capture how she felt on the best day of her life, the day she walked down the aisle with James.

She manages to hold on to the joy of her big day until the end of the song, then reality hits hard, bringing forth sadness and tears. There is no need for Roisin to search out her wedding photos. Her prized moments sit perfectly positioned in the entrance and dining room of her home, evoking the day's wonderful triumph each time she enters and leaves her home. Having spent most of her adult life reconciling herself to the fact that love and marriage were beyond her reach, marrying at the age of fifty-two was a monumental achievement.

Roisin thinks back to a time before, when she saw James as just another stranger. Her hands had rubbed, rolled and danced over almost every part of him, only in the therapeutical sense, every week for five years. She was unnervingly familiar with every contour of his body, the proud curve of his firm, meaty bubble butt, the size of his feet, how hairy his legs were and how the dark hair on his chest tapered neatly to meet the vertical, happy trail teasing her eye towards the mound and exit pocket in his Tommy John's boxer shorts. The moment he arrived, his deep, velvety voice and hardy laugh filled the reception area and beyond. His signature Panama hat was always the first item he removed.

Soon after meeting James for the first time, she considered him to be suave, energetic, pedantic and edgy. She came to rely financially on his attendance at the private physiotherapy clinic in Solihull where she had worked for seven years. In effect, his frequent visits alone paid her mortgage. She had a wobble each time he went overseas, and at the thought he might find a better sports massage therapist. He was her most valued client and, to him, she was physical and emotional stress release, a calm eighty-minute break from having to give of himself and say anything other than a polite greeting and an impersonal goodbye. It did not go unnoticed that he drove a very expensive car and dressed in very exclusive attire. Despite her curiosity, she remained clinical and professional, and respected the quiet he needed. She was reminded of his marital status each time she mobilised and massaged his left hand.

Unlike many other male clients, James never once uttered a flirtatious word or sent a lingering gaze in her direction. From the initial consultation, she knew he was a property developer and owner of Grove House, a care home for the elderly in Solihull, which was part of the Evergreen health group. Their head office was situated a few streets away from the clinic where she worked. It was a time of emotional and physical stress for Roisin in the spring of 2009, due to an acrimonious and drawn-out breakup with Andreas, her partner of fourteen years. She was in survival mode and even though she was already working forty hours a week as a physiotherapist, twenty in the NHS and twenty in the private sector, she needed a further twenty hours, preferably in elderly care, as it was not possible to secure a mortgage on a fifty per cent self-employed income. Her goal was to secure a full-time post in NHS Elderly Community Care, for which she needed further experience.

She thought of Grove House and decided to approach James, who at the time was unsure why a qualified physiotherapist would want to work as a carer for two nights over the weekend. For a year, Roisin worked sixty hours a week. Her life was a mess. She was completely exhausted and emotionally drained. In response to a personal plea from the manager of Grove House, Roisin agreed reluctantly to work an extra day shift on Thursday, her only day off. Mid-morning, while clearing up the aftermath of breakfast, she collapsed in a heap on the dining-room floor. After coming round and throwing up, she was assisted to the manager's office, where she sat with her head over her arms on the desk, stressed and sobbing.

She was a physical wreck, her hair a greasy tangled mess, her face red, puffy and wet with tears, and she smelt of sick. Then in walked James, stuffing a cheeseburger in his mouth.

'Oh crikey,' he mumbled, with a shocked expression, while trying to negotiate a mouthful of meat, cheese and bread, 'it's you …. I forgot you got a job here,' he said, looking her up and down, noticing she was wearing a purple care assistant uniform, rather than her white physiotherapist tunic.

Roisin felt embarrassed, but unable to hold back, continued to sob and splurge out very quickly over the next few minutes the details of her breakup with Andreas, and why she was working every spare hour of every day. James, surprised and usually ham-fisted when faced with a crying woman, put his hand gently on her shoulder, saying in a soft and discreet tone, 'I know how you're feeling. I'm going through a divorce. I'm keeping it under wraps for now as I don't want the staff getting jittery. You go home and get some rest. I'll talk to the manager … Oh, and if you need to cancel my massage appointment on Wednesday, give me a call.'

The following week, on Wednesday at three-thirty, James was sat in the reception waiting room reading the *Daily Mail* as usual. At the sight of Roisin, he rose enthusiastically to his feet.

'Well, you're looking so much brighter than the last time I saw you,' James acknowledged in a spirited and jolly manner.

'Yes, I am brighter, thank you, and for many reasons ... I would like to apologise for the drama in your office. It was unfortunate and out of character,' Roisin replied matter of factly, trying not to come across as squirming and needy. James, usually undressing in haste at this point and diving onto the couch, stopped in his tracks, their eyes locked together in mutual understanding,

'Really, there is no need for an apology, Roisin. Life is a journey of crises and successes. For both of us there are better times ahead.' A warm smile was shared between them.

From that moment on, for six months, every Wednesday on her couch, for the first five minutes, they cogitated about the whys and wherefores of extracting oneself from a crumbling relationship, and how to emerge sane. Roisin began to look forward to Wednesday afternoon and their shared words of support and his amusing anecdotes. He revealed just enough of himself to leave her interested and wanting to know more. As their conversations touched more on who they were, beyond their personal tragedy, she sensed an intrigue swell between them, one of curiosity and possibility. Every Wednesday she thought to herself, 'It can't be him. Of all the men, why are you having thoughts about him? He is not for you. You are lonely. Just be alone.' Roisin tried to reason with herself. 'Please, not another man who is burdened with all the baggage of divorce and hurt. He has teenage sons. He is an older man. For goodness sake, don't make the same mistake again. You need someone who is free at heart, a clean slate and able to give of themselves fully. That's if you need anyone in your life at all.' Her wise words always faded in the moment. While James lay on her couch, his eyes closed, his body relaxed and pliable to her touch, Roisin's eyes explored the shape of his mouth, noticing for the first time that it was in fact rather plummy and inviting and framed by a pretentiously well-groomed dark brown goatee beard. His mostly dark, with a sprinkling of salt and pepper, thick hair, with its messy, playful fringe raised over his hair line, suggested a boyish charm.

Over time, her hands moved more slowly, deeply and sensuously over his body. The occasional curling of his lips, sharp intake of breath and releasing sighs indicated to her his growing pleasure and satisfaction at her expert manipulation. Roisin enjoyed her control as he lay there, a victim of her imagination. Before James was left alone to dress, she stared into his dark chocolate-brown eyes, searching for his thoughts, the intense look exchanged between them revealing their mutual need and inclination.

After enduring a challenging interview process, Roisin secured a thirty-hour week as a team-lead community physiotherapist at Solihull Hospital in Lode Lane, which enabled her to buy a three-bedroom Victorian terrace in Castle Lane. Finally she had a home that was beautifully renovated, complete with old-world charm, and immediately felt as comforting as a loyal friend.

One lovely Sunday morning she was looking forward to taking Twiglet to the park. She recalled telling James at his last appointment where she would be, and she was secretly hoping he had picked up on her cue to turn up and have coffee with her. She decided to wear a short, green, sleeveless summer dress, thinking that if James happened to be there, having seen her in nothing but her work tunic and trousers, he would notice her long, shapely and well-toned bare legs. She left her long, wavy, red hair loose and swaying, feeling this was a much more sensual look.

Roisin was enjoying her walk in the park as she usually did, but this time she felt on edge. She was surprised how much she wanted to see James walking towards her. She was longing to be with him and was not prepared for disappointment. She was wandering around the lake, admiring the beauty of the gliding swans, when suddenly, she caught sight of James walking with a grey Weimaraner. It seemed he did get the message. Feeling elated, she picked up her stride.

'Oh, hello, it's you, James, ... and your dog,' she said, stuttering, a little stuck for words.

'Yes, his name is Blade, I decided the best thing we could do on a lovely Sunday morning was go for a walk in the park. What a coincidence, bumping into you ... and your dog Twiglet, if I remember right?'

'Yes, well remembered,' Roisin said, feeling herself blush. 'What a coincidence,' she affirmed.

'Fancy a coffee?' James suggested, confidently.

'Why not?' Roisin replied with a smug expression plastered on her face.

By the end of the afternoon, after much flirtation, and having realised that they were contagiously encouraging and open-minded to the prospect of an illicit liaison, they parted after confirming an arrangement. He would be arriving at her house the following morning at eight-thirty to take her for an overnight stay in London.

Roisin lay awake most of the night, tossing and turning, her mind and heart racing, enthused by what the next day might or might not bring. At first light, she began the ritual of cleansing, coiffuring, trimming, smoothing and slipping into something slinky and sophisticated. She left a voicemail message at the therapy office, complete with croaky voice and sickly overtones, expressing why she was unable to come into work for a few days. The only thing she was sure of was that she was not backing out. She had a need to be reckless, to act on impulse rather than reason. She had done the right thing and toed the line for far too long; now she had to fly in the face of correctness and good behaviour. 'Oh God,' she said to herself, biting her bottom lip, suddenly erring on the side of doubt.

Just as she lifted her jacket and overnight suitcase, a loud hooting of a car horn sounded twice outside her house. She took one last look at herself, checked for lipstick on her teeth, twirled her fringe out of her eyes, and hoped for the best. On opening her front door, she was faced with James looking very handsome in dark jeans and a navy Corneliani cashmere jacket. Roisin was relieved to see he was also wearing the most delightful mischievous smile, that told her he wanted her.

As he took her heavy bag from her hand and placed it in the boot, nothing was said between them, though their widened smiles and reaching gaze remained connected. She tried her best to hop into the passenger seat with a measure of elegance and dignity, ensuring she did not tear her favourite, just above-the-knee, Max Mara silk cream dress. 'We are really doing this,' she told herself, trembling with excitement, from her imaginings to her pussoir, as she watched James click in his seatbelt, throw her a wink, and a libidinous wolf 'no escape, I got you now, grrrr ... you look delicious' comment.

'You know what this means now, James,' Roisin said, with a sassy smile.

'Go on,' James replied, having no clue as to the question's connotation.

'I will have to recommend you visit Helda with the big muscles for your weekly massages from now on.'

'Oh God,' said James, pulling a face. 'I had better turn around at the next junction.'

Roisin, feeling a little more relaxed, was now sure her recently purchased Rosie Huntington-Whiteley ivory panties and suspender set would not go unappreciated. The journey to the Chesterfield Mayfair hotel was filled with sexual innuendos, supposition and youthful frivolity. Roisin was surprised to see the doorman was dressed in a red waistcoat and black tie and thought he greeted James with distinct familiarity as he retrieved their bags from the boot of his car.

The hotel entrance doors were opened by another smartly prinked gentleman, tilting his hat respectfully.

'Shall I park your car, Mr Landry,' he enquired subserviently, reaching out an upturned hand. Roisin was very impressed by the attentive service at the hotel. She looked up and around, admiring the high ceilings, the traditional floor-to-ceiling mirrored glass, ornate brass doorknobs and hanging chandeliers, among other Victorian features, which spoke of a gentlemen's smoking room, an 1800s bygone era, one which she felt James fit seamlessly into.

Roisin, standing in the shadows, her mind now apprehensively thinking of what would come next, a touch, a kiss, the bed; and a hunch that the fleeting glances discreetly directed towards her by personnel suggested she was one of many women to be allured by James into the Duchess Suite. With a clinking of the door key in his hand, the wolf wet his lips, placed his hand in the small of her back, preparing his feast for undressing and mauling with his hungering eyes. Roisin, her potency now weakened by his prowess, for the first time felt vulnerable, like prey. The plush deep red carpet led them to the Duchess Suite.

As they opened the door, the bell boy noisily brought in their luggage, interrupting the heightening tension between them. Roisin, aware she was holding her breath, feigning confidence, and anticipating the moment he would vacate their room, needed a shot of something strong to inhibit the fluster. She clocked the bottle of champagne, two glasses and a bouquet of flowers on the round table by the window. The closing of the door brought her attention back to James. They stood together in the middle of the room, eyes flickering tensely, gauging who would make the first move. They reached out and linked hands, sensually massaging each other's palms and fingers. In sync, they took a step closer towards one another.

'You know my body so well. Your hands have been almost everywhere,' James remarked candidly, smirking, reminding her of her advantage.

'The irony of it,' Roisin proclaimed, flicking her head and raising her eyebrows. 'I am the one at a disadvantage here, I am the one with the most to reveal.' Looking in the direction of the champagne, she breathed out heavily. 'I need a drink.' Before she could turn her head round, James had the sides of her face in his hands, and his mouth pressing into hers. Wrapping one arm around her waist, he pulled her forcefully into his body, his mouth vigorously working in and over her lips, down her neck and into her cleavage. He took her breath away, the need for him to touch her, and take her, soared within her.

'You slinky, spicy, irresistible cocktail of lust,' James said in a deep, husky, velvety voice, grabbing her peachy firm bottom in both his hands, lifting her off the floor in one swift move and taking hold under her thighs, jolting her legs around his hips.

Roisin gripped her legs around him, while grasping and pulling at his hair with one hand, and steadying her position on his leather trouser belt with the other. James launched himself on the Savoir emperor-sized bed, careful not to land harshly on top of her. She instantly felt the deep pleasure and satisfaction of his strength and hardness pounding onto her body, his gyrating thrusts and roving hands raising her silky dress, exposing her ivory slip of a thong and firm round buttocks. He slipped his fingers expertly under her thong, and down into her warm welcoming space. Her plumpness tensed and pulsated over his fingers, as he wandered through to the deeper parts of her, his thumb skilfully teasing her love bud, causing her to jut up and forward, further into his aching rock-hard length, hammering for release.

In a moment of rough handling, her dress was torn, revealing her firm breasts adorned in ivory silk, and suddenly his cock was free and finding its way to her sweet spot. Roisin writhed in ecstasy, her whole body wanting him to take her hard and fast. She dug her nails hard into his buttocks and under his shirt, upwards clawing into his back. Suddenly James rose up, and dived down between her legs. Proficient with his tongue, he took her to the edge of orgasm.

'Every woman deserves a man who loves to eat her out,' James declared, his head raised up between her thighs, his mouth and face wet with her moistness, divulging his voracious appetite.

Roisin answered, her words breathy, 'You are my wolf, you can see me better, hear me better and eat me with such savagery.' She lost herself, her head thrown from side to side, her body ridged, arcing with intense pleasure … James took his moment, thrusting himself hard and fast with all his strength into her hot eruption, back and forth, driving deep into her, through her gasps and screams, until the silence became deafening … until they were fulfilled and released. 'We kissed for the first time today, but I have longed for that kiss for some time,' Roisin whispered to James, running her fingers through his fringe. She kissed him tenderly. 'You taste so good,' she said, closing her eyes and drifting into a contented sleep. Embraced, they awoke together with no regrets, only a need to enjoy the warmth and closeness of each other's skin and smell.

The following weekends spent together in London's hot spots were crammed with exhilaration, intimate pleasure and, for Roisin, newly found top-dollar experiences. Roisin proved herself to be a natural when performing the role of delicious seductress draped over a rich man's arm, shrewdly massaging his intellectual ego, and flirting outrageously. She played the part of the agreeable tart with expertise, satisfying the needs of her pay master, a small price to pay she thought, for partaking in high-society elitist extravagance and sumptuous Michelin-star dining. She was a small frog in a big pond but now felt more worthy and noticed. With each day that passed, her mind and appetite were aroused by the tastes and pleasures enjoyed by the well-heeled and disgustingly rich. It only took five days and four nights of luxuriated ruination, and she was unreservedly sold on the notion that she would no longer accept a life of denial and serfdom.

There were moments when what she experienced and touched felt real and tangible, but she dared not imagine it as anything other than fleeting, and already a memory, one which was imaginary, and not hers to cherish and recall at will. Her newly attained persona was very much dependent on attending to the whimsical needs of James and abiding to a semblance of the woman in his dreams, for as long as he wanted her. She admired James's ability to move freely in the mix of grime and glamour, his perceptive intellect, and convincing gentlemanly persuasions; altogether, an edgy, charming and gold-plated formula, one she knew many women found appealing in a man.

Roisin hoped she was firmly entrenched in his mind. When she found herself alone with James on a privately chartered yacht, during a week's holiday in Portofino, she sensed a wooing of hearts between them. They strolled hand in hand on the beach, swooshing through the warm frothy white sea with their bare feet. They could be a couple in love, she thought to herself. One dusky evening, James, dressed in a sea-blue linen shirt, smart cream trousers, Crockett & Jones loafers and, as always, his Bates of London Panama hat, held her hand tenderly, and cast her a ready-to-please smile and gaze, suggesting his delight in her company.

Adorned in a flouncy chiffon peach off-the-shoulder dress and chic sandals, Roisin sashayed proudly alongside her man, arriving at the Ristorante Puny for a dining experience on the romantically lit harbour's edge. They sat close together, still able to hold hands and affectionately touch. James kissed her sultrily on the lips, a kiss that said, 'I want you in my days and not just a secret lust for my nights.' They both opened their eyes at the sound of the sommelier clearing his throat with urgency.

'Sir, Madame,' he pronounced decisively, 'we have flames rising from your table!' Springing into action, he grabbed a fork and positioned it under the lip of the Panama hat. With one fell swoop, he flicked the burning Panama up into the air and onto the pavement. James, with his index finger pushed into his upper lip, shot a surprised look at Roisin.

'Crikey, I must have put it down on a candle! That's three thousand pounds up in smoke in seconds,' he said, screwing up his face.

'Oh, darling, shall we cancel the Dom Perignon?' Roisin suggested, with a disconcerted look and a hand on his knee.

'Not at all,' James replied resolutely, attempting to disguise a grimace, while flitting between admiring the exceptional pageantry of super yachts and his disappointment at the sight of his Panama hat shrivelling to a blackened carcass.

After a charming week's stay at the 1950s-style Belmond Splendido Hotel and five days sailing on a luxury yacht in the sun with James, Roisin sensed a new chapter ahead. A bold and beautiful phoenix rising from the ashes of her charred and deathly existence, a most unexpected journey waiting before her. She could see a warm and alluring glow, beckoning promise, joyous frivolity and even love. She feared an ordinary life would from now on seem dull.

Over the months that followed, James provided the glitz and the glamour in her free time. Long weekends in Dubai, and in Monaco, an excursion and meal at Buckingham Palace, various London theatre shows, the Royal Variety Performance and a romantic weekend in Paris. It was all very much in the fast lane, first class, and back to work and Twiglet by the skin of her teeth. Exhausting, but addictive. As lovers, they enjoyed the exhilaration of exploring one another without any fear of unrequited love. But Roisin sensed that the passion and novelty of their coming together would fizzle out in due course. Roisin acknowledged to herself that they were both licking their wounds and finding solace in each other's story.

She felt damaged by the demise of her relationship with Andreas but was essentially free to run away with her emotions, her desires in the moment. Her time was her own. James, however, was at the helm of a vast business and was a father of two teenage boys, Ethan and Noah, and an older son Gabriel, who was born when James was twenty years old and married to his first wife, Marie, who sadly passed away in her early forties.

James was also deeply entrenched in the throes of an acrimonious divorce from the mother of his two younger sons. Roisin had labelled herself 'the sticking plaster', which he would discard, once he was emotionally strong and able to seek out his true love, his equal. For now, Roisin was going along for the ride, taking in the rush and embracing the urgency of life. James had told her he was hell-bent on packing out his bucket list; he often quoted Ashley Montagu: 'The idea is to die young as late as possible.' Roisin sensed that life with James might offer endless opportunities and fun, just what she needed in her life right now. Having her heart broken along the way, she feels is a risk worth taking.

The present, Friday, 7.30 p.m.

Roisin, suddenly woken by the ring tone on her phone, hurriedly scrambles around with her hands, feeling under her pillow and blankets, but misses the call. She had fallen asleep with thoughts of her wedding day on her mind, the image of herself in her ivory dress swirling in slow motion, while she danced to the sound of the song 'Roxanne'. Roisin glances over towards a black-and-white photo that sits on her dressing table, her most treasured image that captured her mood and thoughts the moment before she married James.

She recalls standing under the ornate white stone archway which was above and around her, framing her image as a halo would an angel in a flowing gown. The sun outside set its white rays behind her, catching the curves and folds of her waist and her movement as she took one tentative step through the open oak door and into the church porch. The train of her ivory wedding dress was puckered and lifted over her right arm to ensure her refinement and togetherness. She bore no smile, only an expression swathed in seriousness, a gathering of her composure, with her focus on only the next step forward to a moment she thought would never be. She remembers sharing a heartfelt glance with Reverend Paul as he stood before her, welcoming her into this quaintest of village churches.

The image is full of enchantment and artistry, and it captures the moment when a woman takes a leap of faith into the house of God and into the fullness of another's heart and life. A promise made, 'je ne sais quoi' amid the alchemy of love. Another photo taken on her wedding day and close to her heart, one she has thought a lot about over the last few days, shows her standing close to James surrounded by both families. In contrast to the first photo, it is bursting with colour and jubilant smiles. Flashes of lavender and purple entwine with the cream and greens of beautiful flowers and pretty leaves, all coming together in bouquets and garlands, elevating the heavenly ambience, expounding all that was perfect in her world.

James turned around and watched his bride as she walked towards him to the sensational voice of Etta James, singing 'At Last' – very fitting for a fifty-two-year-old spinster who thought she would never be addressed as Mrs, or my wife. Their broadening smiles reflected their heartful need and the honesty of their commitment.

Her bespoke wedding dress, designed by her own mind's eye, took eight months to create. Her makeup had been perfected, her teeth whitened, and her hair fashioned early that morning by her trusted hairdresser. Every moment and movement of the day was rehearsed, yet the overwhelming feeling and emotion of its monumental meaning only surfaced on her wedding day. Every word heard and spoken, and every smile and glance that came her way, was as special as anything could have ever been for her. With Darra by her side, handsome and delighted to be giving her away, her moment was complete. Orla, her girls, Annie and Jemma and James's granddaughter Henrika, were bridesmaids. Elof, James's grandson was pageboy and all Darra's children and James's family were present. The wedding service was very much plucked from the pages of the Bible. It was formal and spiritual, and she felt her God came to visit her that day for the very best of reasons.

The reception, held in a huge marquee in the grounds of Landry's Lair, with all its finery, premier catering, and Bryan Ferry and Roxy music tribute band was everything and more than she had dreamed of. Roisin not even once had a moment of nerves or doubt, her smile never left her and when she saw tears of joy swell in the eyes of her husband-to-be as they gave their vows, she knew she was at last loved. They honeymooned at the Hotel George V in Paris and immersed themselves in the culture and wonder of the city of romance. Hand in hand, entwined as one, she finally knew where love could take you.

A text message on her phone brings her back to reality with a jolt. It's from James. 'Hello, my darling, missing you, and wondering why you haven't contacted me?' Placing the phone on her chest, Roisin takes in a deep breath, closing her eyes. She knows no contact is her only option right now.

Roisin was never any good at lying. Her dumbed-down voice and lack of enthusiasm will give away her mood. James is smart and she knows she will crack under interrogation. She needs more time alone. On hearing Jax and Coco barking in the distance and feeling faint from lack of food, she pulls herself together, peeling herself away from trying to reconcile the joy of her wedding day with the fear of losing James and her secure existence. She places both her hands on the oak and gun-metal staircase of the galleried landing, perusing the vast and open space below.

Her eyes trace the curves and lines of the ceiling structure down to the lounge, dining and kitchen areas. She reflects sombrely on this house they designed and built together – a place that became her home and holds so many family memories. The thought of those memories continuing without her fills her with sadness. She can no longer fight back the tears.

She steps into Ethan's bedroom, tidy only because he's in America and Sandra, the housekeeper, has picked up his clothes and cleared away the empty pizza boxes – tasks Roisin refuses to do herself and usually tells Sandra not to do. She recalls the times when he was young and thought nothing of hugging her affectionately while sharing a tub of popcorn and watching a film.

She walks past Noah's room and stops. She hesitates, trying to remember the last time she went in there. It must be at least six weeks, longer for James. She turns around and opens his door. She is not expecting any surprises. It will look and feel the same as it did ten months ago, after he took his own life. Without Noah, it is empty and lifeless. Roisin looks straight ahead at the far wall as she always did, at the large, beautifully framed photo collage on the wall. A moment in time when Noah, Ethan, Dad and Mum were happy together as one family: the smiles, the frolicking, the artistry of a playful loving family captured at the click of a camera. Their mother, Talia, looks gorgeous with her long, dark, shiny hair and warm eyes, her body wrapped dotingly around her young children, and James looking so proud and protective of his family. A perfect beginning, so much of everything, yet it ended in tragedy.

Roisin takes herself for a 'wake up and clear your head' shower, and then walks into the shared dressing room for a change of clothes. Her side of the dressing room is a palate of colours and designs of every description. She does not have a specific style. If it looks good with her long auburn hair, and flatters her figure, she can fall in love with any brand or price tag. She often finds her most surprising and treasured items when on a charity-shop tour, something James would never contemplate.

She turns around and is faced with rows of samey coordinated clothing. With James no longer in the house and now that all she is thinking about, day and night, is leaving him, and what her life might look like without him, it is his clothes that bring her closer to him. She finds herself staring at the contents of his side of the dressing room with raised eyebrows, recalling the film *Sleeping with the Enemy*. She ponders its ending. She knows the tins of beans and soups, etc. lined up on the pantry shelves remain chaotic and random, but she always knew that if she ever saw them in uniform lines, like soldiers waiting on inspection, her brow would begin to perspire. She knew he was a perfectionist when they first met, but his obsessive-compulsive disorder when it comes to routine and wearing the same clothes has taken on new meaning. It now defines who he is.

She lifts the cuff on a shirt and takes in his smell. Only one make of shirt, a Turnbull & Asser striped dress shirt, of which he has thirty, grouped according to colour and then thickness of stripe, hanging on the rail. There are twenty Moss custom-made trousers and suits, non-shiny and only in black or dark blue. When James is informal, which is rare these days, she mostly sees him in a short-sleeved plain cotton shirt, of which there are two colour options. Roisin has given up introducing her husband to variety in clothing accepting that he should be himself, not her version of him.

5

THE HONEY, MONEY POT

Roisin, feeling the need for fresh air, wanders into the garden. She looks at the pétanque pitch and recalls the many light-hearted competitions and laughter she and James have shared with their friends. She remembers fretting each month as she attempted to reach the giddy heights of Stepford, perfect wife status, because James insisted on hosting a four-course gourmet French meal after their game of boules. A smile comes to her face as she thinks of how proud James was when his friends named him *Le President*. James loves everything French, including Amélie, her friend.

Roisin knows her husband is impressed by Amélie, and she has often felt jealous, wishing she could speak French and flaunt her sassiness in the same way. Amélie is a slim and toned salacious siren, and she knows it. Roisin believes Amélie is very much in love with her husband, Leo, but now that it has become apparent infidelity is James's modus operandi, she wonders if he only has a partiality for Russian girls, or if he has already bedded his French fancy, or if she were out of the way, would Amélie very quickly take her place.

James is overwhelmed by love and friendships, and Roisin is very aware that all his friends have become her friends. He has given something so important to her, this priceless joy that she found unattainable throughout most of her life. Now she has an ocean of friends, amazing and wonderful friends, and feels like the Posh in the Posh and Becks of Barston village.

Roisin is proud of her husband's generosity with his money. She knows he loves nothing more than playing a part in fulfilling everyone's dreams, and she also knows this would not change if she were no longer with him. His life would continue to be fully enriched and she feels, for him, little would change. She does wonder how her friends would negotiate their way around her if she were single. She is sure she would become less relevant, a sticking point and no longer a good fit within their world of coupledom. She knows her friends would welcome her replacement, and she would have to step aside, just as James's ex-wife Talia had to, when she jumped into her shoes. Roisin feels the need to take herself back through some of their good times. She wants to think about what she is giving up, the things that she will miss. She feels lucky to have jumped on the gravy train at a time when James's bucket list was overflowing and he was driving at full pelt. She just wishes she could keep up with the pace.

From fairly early stages – aged twenty, living in a caravan, married with a two-year-old – his propensity for devising adventures and amassing monetary success had taken an upward trajectory. His decisive business acumen and compulsion for future advancement have remained steadfast and lucrative, and now he is an enigmatic multi-millionaire with love in his heart, James Landry can see an unexpected future ahead. For Roisin, her every worldly desire lay in the palm of her hand. Her fingers, like a billowing cloud cushioning tempestuous winds, cautiously protected her good fortune. It was all hers to feel, to taste. The rewards were limitless: infinite holidays and an overflowing vibrant social circle tasting every splendid luxury and experience that money can buy.

The best veal chop and zabaglione savoured in the warm teasing breeze of Porto Cervo, the exquisite delights created by the master, Michel Roux Jr at the eternally romantic Le Gavroche, and the traditionally French Boudin Blanc in Mayfair serving garlic with frogs' legs, garlic with escargot, garlic with everything. And then some ... On and on, tasting the gastronomy of the finest in the world, fulfilling James's mission to dine at every Michelin-star restaurant before he meets his maker, and fulfilling Roisin's wildest dreams. And the dreams came true at a hurtling rate. It was and is a head spin.

'Honey, darling,' James would say before everything, 'Andrea Bocelli is performing in Rome. Honey, I've booked the Albert Hall again ... Oh and don't forget we are leaving for Dubai at the weekend ... the Atlantis this time. Oh, honey, cancel whatever you are doing in May. Four weeks sailing booked around the Adriatic and Med with Roland and Bong-cha. That should be interesting now you've passed your competent crew course. The train journey to the Jungfraujoch in Switzerland as part of our summer European tour in a month's time, honey. If that ice ledge is good enough for James Bond, it's good enough for James Landry.'

'Gabriel and Freja have set a wedding date in Sweden next September. After visiting the Vasa ship in Stockholm, it's just a hop and a skip across to Copenhagen and we are in the Baltic Sea. We should visit St Petersburg and Moscow and say hi to Putin. Machu Picchu and the Galapagos next year with the boys and, of course, one for your bucket list, honey, Sri Lanka. And you get to wash a baby elephant … ah … how good will that be?' And it was perfect – her most memorable moment, watching a great herd of elephants, ears flapping, their huge bodies thundering through the village and heading as one family down to the fast-flowing river below. In a still pool, the babies were brought to play and be washed by ecstatic tourists. It was the most transcendent experience.

That day, James fulfilled her lifelong wish and then topped it off with an unimaginable feat of love. He ordered a life-size wooden baby elephant and had it shipped to their home address. It arrived in a huge wooden crate which only just fit into the garage space; it weighed a ton. She came home from work and stood in front of the monstrous crate; she was flabbergasted by what she saw and what she imagined. At any moment, she expected what was inside to start growling or trumpeting and bashing the sides, desperate to get out. It took six men and farm equipment to land the elephant in the wooded area of Landry's Lair where it would live forever, reminding her every day of James's spontaneous act of love.

A different sort of reveal popped up in full view from their mini cruise ship cabin window when they left St

Petersburg behind and sailed close by a titanic pile of military ships and submarines before slipping into the Baltic Sea. To their surprise, Putin was not attempting to hide his arsenal of war.

The constant packing and unpacking were relentless. James could work from anywhere on his laptop and phone. Long after they were married and James became chairman of his company, and more acutely aware of his age and the speed of his years passing by, he ramped up the socialising and travelling schedule, with private jets to avoid the stress of fast track, helicopter rides, chauffeurs, anything to avoid wasting time. Roisin's social life was no longer in her control and became incompatible with working even two days a week. So, she retired, aged fifty-six, and attempted, through menopausal hot flushes, brain fog, a hysterectomy and a knee replacement, to keep up with the sprightly, never-an-off-button husband James.

Always leaving the house by the skin of her teeth, late and exhausted, while reassuring, 'No, darling, of course I haven't forgotten to pack your Panama hat, how on earth would I find you if I did?' And in between the far-flung destinations there were the never-ending London trips, the shows, the Royal Variety Performance and after-party, the British TV awards; the best sushi and champagne at Harrods, the best afternoon tea and evening caviar and champagne experience at The Ritz. Henley Regatta, Centre Court Wimbledon and the Grand Prix, always with top hospitality; the Hebridean Princess and Scottish tours and the long weekends and stays around the United Kingdom. She was, and is a very privileged and lucky puss, as her husband likes to call her; although, granted, she is also an exhausted woman. All their closest twenty-four friends, twelve couples for different events, have brought different moods and conversation to their life in the fast lane.

Roisin is very aware that what sits in her husband's head typically splurges out unfiltered, sometimes to her disappointment. She knows he is not always so magnanimous, but she did always think he was faithful. He is famed for his outspoken, 'give it to them straight' approach, an attitude that she and friends alike have accepted, and continue to graciously skirt around. She recalls a profusion of 'only priority fast track will do, it's not quite Dom Perignon, sunny side up please, lightly cooked, preferably gooier than firm, coffee a must-have, uncompromisingly, only his preference in taste and strength will suffice, too elite, too kingly and "Do they not know who I am?" He was now firmly of that ilk.

Roisin has come to realise of late that James is intrinsically unable to swallow sub-standard, just make-do, pizza for dinner, or the 'pleb class'. Feeling slightly threadbare while trying to keep up with his standards, she has always admired that he knows want he likes and wants, but when her tolerance is low, it can be wearing. Roisin remembers one such flaunt kicked off while they were grabbing a last gin and tonic in the business class lounge on their travels to the Caribbean island of Grenada.

Roisin, while tightly squeezed between James and both grandchildren, agitatedly regurgitated her fraught risk assessment of the dilapidated helicopter's performance from the hotel and descent into Hewanorra Airport in St Lucia, wondering why on earth James had booked such an outmoded form of transport. Every second of the long-drawn-out flight parodied huddling together, looking out from the insides of an aged wasp. As the helicopter spewed out its creaks and groans and spluttered to its landing spot, it felt like the culmination of a doomed, ugly twist of fate had just been avoided.

James, noticing his wife's distress, robustly proclaimed it all an exciting, successful jaunt that had avoided two hours of driving, and was therefore a smart move. Roisin knew he was a risk taker but was exasperated that his whole family also had to endure this risk. Roisin watched Freja, his Swedish daughter-in-law, usually the personification of calm, find her inner Viking, ferociously scoop up her children and join her husband Gabriel, Ethan and Noah, James's three sons and, head shell-shocked to British Airways departures where they would later board a flight to the United Kingdom.

Roisin, following behind James, marched on at speed, seeking out the British Airways VIP lounge, in readiness for a twenty-five-minute 'proper plane' hop to the luxury boutique Calabash Hotel, nuzzled in Prickly Bay, Grenada. Once comfortably settled, time took on a different pace. Roisin remembers sitting next to her husband and taking a moment to study him closely.

He was slumped in a chair, legs crossed, his knuckles pushing his cheek and mouth upward in an unattractive, scrunched-up manner, only just visible under the rim of his Panama hat. He was immersed in his iPad, and oblivious to her scrutiny. She lurched closer, peering over his shoulder. By his own admission, he had been a long time absent as his head was gummed up in the *Daily Mail*'s report on Conservative party shenanigans, presently post-pandemic petty feuding and indiscriminate bloodletting, while feverishly teetering on the edge of the nuclear annihilation of Conservatism. Roisin knew James had his wager firmly on 'Bo Jo' remaining PM.

Politics is James's preferred subject of debate, and Roisin is convinced her husband's political persuasion is down to 'Boris's gusto' and the plethora of jokey blokey banter that is teleported daily into his private office. She, on the other hand, made it clear to her husband at the hustings that she believed it was political suicide to endorse a man who left his car and his wife and family in chaos to run the country. James pointed out to her that it is his philandering that sticks in her gut, and that that should not matter a jot, or be a deal-breaker. Roisin remembers looking at James in disbelief at how quickly he dismissed his hero's selfish pursuit of affairs and the abandonment of his loved ones. James's attitude that boys will be boys had begun to give her cause for concern.

Roisin, delighted with her two recently purchased, duty-free, soft, vibrant blue cushions-cum-blankets, 'designed to enhance one's flight experience', attached them to their cabin case. James, having come to expect all things top-notch, was horrified, and spent the next twenty minutes demonising and disparaging them, and obsessively reiterating that it was a 'cringe-worthy, humiliating walk of shame', wheeling his Tumi hand luggage into business class with what he called 'council estate wallers', dole dippers', park-bench blockers' furry dice stuff' attached. He ordered her to 'Get rid!' Roisin, very happy with her 'furry dice', considered it all to be a pompous drama and unnecessary.

Continuing to scowl and glaring from the furry dice to Roisin throughout the duration of settling into BA's comfy sleeping pods, James decided to raise the central screen divider to avoid the Celtic stare. A juvenile five-minute up-and-down duel then ensued until Roisin could no longer contain her cynical laughter. After she declined the welcoming glass of champagne, the dashing, flamboyantly 'out there' steward presented Roisin with a silver tray carrying a packet of nuts, questioning curiously, 'Would you like some spicy nuts then?'

'No thank you,' she replied, shifting her gaze towards James. 'I already have two sitting next to me.' With pouting lips and raised eyebrows, the tittering gentleman sauntered off.

Roisin thought everything about the Calabash Hotel was exquisite. The cabana where they stayed was adorned in pastel tones throughout, the open floor-to-ceiling windows were framed with sheer white linen curtains that danced with the warm breeze. Roisin took in the vision of tropical flowers, pure white sand and silky rolling waves caressed by a blue sky and a warm golden haze that tempted her each morning from her bed. Just as memorable was the Hobie Cat experience. Roisin recalls her time-critical role as strategic ballast, floundering and rolling over on all fours, grabbing the sail pulley rope tight, while tacking and negotiating the swing direction of the boom. She knew it was not a pretty sight, but worth the rip-roaring laugh with James.

Not so funny for her was a snorkelling trip to the Molinere Underwater Sculpture Park. Roisin sat perched on the edge of the boat, pinching her nose, next in line to be flipped over into the choppy sea. Looking down through the tightly fitted Perspex and rubber goggles sucking her face, she saw that she was the only one wearing bright canary-yellow flippers. James soon found her flapping above the water, readjusting her snorkel, spluttering the need to change her flippers. She remembers he looked exasperated, thinking they were the wrong size. She was terrified, thinking that, to a shark, her flapping propellers were a glowing beacon, screaming dinner.

On entering the salty abyss, a deep black eeriness shrouded the guileless Roisin. She found the experience frightfully unnerving. She was besieged by the surround sound of deafening crackles and undulating murmurings which alerted her to the encircling teem of life. Her senses were overloaded. She was relieved to feel James catching hold of her hand. Her imagination was savage. Suddenly, the mouth of a great white blasted out of the foggy depths, ripping her face off – she knew she should have changed those damn flippers. She squeezed James's hand a little harder. Having become a little more accustomed to her watery world, and bolstered by a thumbs up from James, Roisin relaxed and put aside her perceived shark attack.

Aged fifty-eight, Roisin thought herself 'rather saucy' as she rolled her eyes over the sultry man, dining alone in the garden of the next-door, private, bamboo cabana. She particularly noticed the crisp white napkin tucked in the neck of his tightly fitted, undoubtedly bespoke, Italian blue silk shirt. The vibrant colours accentuated his tan, and his manly porn-star pectorals; she was surprised by how a three-second glance could elicit so much in her mind's eye: his need of her attention, their first passionate embrace and lustful liaison – and she hit the replay button at least twice. Only a slight distraction interrupting her few steps to breakfast on the beach, she thought, smiling to herself. She picked up the pace, catching up with the impatient James, and slipped her hand sensually into his. Roisin took a moment to breathe in the warm sea air and admire the beach. This place was her paradise, a place bestowing rejuvenation and a time spent re-discovering the reasons why the love between herself and James made sense.

Despite many holiday romances, their relationship had succumbed to reality – the daily grind, nagging frustrations, and conversations that never quite happened. With each year and deepening familiarity, rows became increasingly frequent, unrestrained and cutting, and negotiating her position within their relationship now felt more of a challenge and thwarting her husband's overbearing presence more of a necessity.

Roisin often relives her first few years with James, the ease with which they melded together, their passion and eagerness to pleasure each other, when sex was a priority, not an afterthought, or a date in the diary. No planning was required; his lustful spontaneity showed her how much he needed and desired her. Now she has a partial knee replacement, hysterectomy hangover, menopausal meltdown, and much hated chub between the thighs, Roisin feels very much undesirable. The fading attention and interest from her husband is worrying her greatly, especially as she feels powerless to stop the ever-widening chasm between them from turning into an empty black hole, one that she can see herself teetering on the edge of, waiting for the moment when she will fall into its barrenness. Roisin wanted to be that couple who always held hands and kept each other close, even when in a crowd, and regardless of the longevity of their lives together, but James does not feel the same need. For Roisin, the little touches say so much more than any grand gesture ever could.

Like many a lonely housewife, she still possesses the yearning inclination, in between attending to the needs of her husband and dutiful domestic chores, to nurture her libido with her friend Black Rod. He understands her needs implicitly, gets on with the job unselfishly and doesn't blab to his friends down the pub. Black Rod, so called after his namesake, the parliamentary basher who allows the ruling of the nation and precedes all important decision-making – a bit like Boris Johnson, the randy PM, preaching from Number 10 while broadening his brood – is her elixir of youth, her energiser and gears the re-setting of her chakras.

Now with James, relations are maturing into the 'Stinking Bishop, overripe cheese and all a bit off' phase, and his tolerance of his wife's occasional Celtic outbursts are beginning to wane. Roisin has come to think his habitual stonking predictability and the last twelve years of cajoling and tutoring her to the point of military mastery in the wants and whims of 'Lord Landry', have left her, maybe foolishly, feeling immune to the possibility of a ceremonial dumping for a younger, non-malfunctioning model.

She finds herself recalling the 'French tart' moment while staring into a cup of tea.

They had always enjoyed a soirée at Le Boudin Blanc, Mayfair, London, their usual preference, before ending the night tumbling fervently onto the delicious, perfectly crisp pillows awaiting them back at the utterly charming Chesterfield Mayfair hotel. But on this occasion Roisin, feeling powerless and less noticed than seabed bottom feeders, but still keen to rouse James's interest in her attributes, observed his protruding chin, resting on his clasped hand, his unblinking, widened eyes fixed wholly on the goddess, awaiting his menu choice. James, continuing to 'graze' over her pert bosom, perfectly peachy posterior and suggestive gesticulations, jolted Roisin to attention. Her 'Stinking Bishop' was still highly susceptible to an alluring liaison – one that undeniably exuded French sultry tones. Meanwhile, Roisin was left feeling disconnected and deactivated.

Her only prospect now for sex hinges on James's ability to enact his fantasy ... with her rival ... he has her silent permission! Roisin, feeling very much 'fully ripened on the vine', has come to believe that every man has a French tart within him, or rather him in her, whether his first love is God almighty, or the luscious Liz Hurley, as in the case of Hugh Grant and his 'Divine, Divine' fellatio affaire.

6

THE HEN HOUSE

The present, Saturday, 9 a.m.

After an unsettled night's sleep, Roisin wakes up late. Realising she is missing a beautiful sunny morning, she opens the double doors in the sunroom, letting in the fresh air and a bounding, hungry Jax and Coco. After feeding the dogs and having a play, she admires the beauty of the garden, recalling the amazing yearly wedding anniversary garden parties, thinking last year's celebration will be their last. She walks into her favourite place in the whole house, her art studio, designed especially for her by James when the house was built. There is a huge easel in the corner with a large oil painting of a young woman, not yet complete, commanding the room with its vibrant contrasting colours and seductive pose.

The vibrant red of her hair, draped over her porcelain neck and shoulders, stands out strikingly against the soft vintage green of the velvet chaise longue – the same one in the corner of the art room. Her favourite place of comfort and familiarity, it is the chaise longue where she has fallen asleep, tired after a long day's work, where she has drunk away her loneliness, her tears draining into its springs. The same chaise longue on which she performed her first striptease in a rapture of confidence and potency while straddling Ian Hayden, her first love, while high and rocking on Southern Comfort. The green velvet chaise longue shares the hallmark of her experience, a reminder of where she has been. Its trials are her trials, its presence has purpose, it retells the good decisions and the bad as it wraps itself around her, leaving her, after much deliberation, with a clear way forward. Despite its fraying and fustiness, it is too precious to discard.

In the painting, her near-naked body lies adrift over the chaise longue, asleep and unaware that the ivory silk of her negligee suggests seduction or even contentment after passion, as it glides over the curve of her upper thighs and down into the triangle of her desire. Her face is turned away from the voyeur, and an empty glass, fallen on its side, tells little of her mood. The Polaroid photo perched in the corner of the easel was taken when she was twenty years old by Ian Hayden, on an evening when he fiercely loved her, then left her to wake up to the cold and stark reality of a dark and lonely night.

Roisin knows she must finish the painting, but knows that this weekend is not the right time. It is, however, the perfect time to call Polly and tell her everything about James and what she is going through. Polly Ripper, a bohemian free-spirited, tree-hugging, ditsy aromatherapist, and Roisin hit it off big time while attending the same aromatherapy training course twenty-four years ago. They both delight in the fact that the geographical distance between them, and their now very differing lifestyles, has not caused them to drift apart. She so wants to come over; Roisin successfully talks her out of it.

'Why didn't you tell me in Marbella?' Polly questions.

'I didn't want to ruin our weekend,' Roisin explains. 'I needed to be sure. I spoke only to Vivi. I needed time to work through everything and make sense of it all.' The two friends cry and laugh together and once they are past the sadness, they reminisce about the magical time they all had in Marbella.

. . .

Seven months after first dating James, one stormy early evening, Roisin tentatively applied her foundation, mascara and lipstick, preparing herself to meet Arrabella and Barnaby Bucks, James's closest friends, for the first time. She knew she had to look her very best, leaving no telltale makeup tide marks under her chin, rogue dark smudges under the eyes, or lip liner veering off-piste, shouting tatty and trailer park. Two minutes away from arriving at their house for an intimate meal for four, James decided to say in a direct, almost combatant way, 'I hope you're not one of those women threatened by the presence of a stunningly beautiful woman.'

'What?' Roisin replied, feeling very put out. 'Why would you say such a thing to me, James? I am not that uncomfortable in my own skin. They either like me, or they don't.'

'Just saying,' James explained, 'Arrabella is gorgeous.'

Roisin fidgeted in the passenger seat of his Bentley,

suddenly feeling underdressed and questioning her choice of outfit. Her fears turned out to be unfounded. What started as a warm and sincere greeting blossomed into a wonderful friendship and, years later, Roisin was thrilled to be sat next to Arrabella, still a glamourous and beautiful woman, and among their besties, champagne in hand, celebrating Arrabella's sixtieth birthday at her luxurious beachside Casa in Marbella.

Arrabella's beachfront house party came with specific rules. She insisted all those invited behave in a way they would have done thirty-five years ago, before children, marriage and the responsibilities of looking after mum and dad.

'No men, no excuse, we go raw and relaxed,' she said. Roisin reaches for the sparkly framed Marbella Beach photo on the shelf in her art room and immediately her melancholic mood lifts at the sight of herself and her friends dressed in their barely there beachwear. Smiling broadly to herself, she recalls the getting drunk together, the rolling around laughing uncontrollably, while their wobbly, bobbly bits burst out of their straining itsy bitsy bikinis ... it was the best of laughs.

Arrabella was so happy. She is always the fiercely protective mama hen, content when her chicks are running around her. She still looks every bit the enchanting model she was in her younger days. Her early-morning runs play their part in keeping her fit. Her dramatic, ice-blonde, hairstyle, electric-blue almond-shaped eyes and petite features give her a striking head-turning look, one that Roisin knows she can only aspire to.

Despite her full-on social life, Roisin manages to visit

Polly with Arrabella at least three times a year at her cottage in the home counties, that is when she is not backpacking with her on-off Spanish lover, Pedro. Then, there are the girlie holidays, the big birthdays, the weddings of each other's children and the 'I need to stay with you for a few days, life is shit, I need a friend' moments. The hens always keep the flame of friendship burning. With age, they have come to know the value of womanhood and all its advantages, engineering free time to have a whinge-fest, talk about nothing and everything, helping guide one another through life, reminding each other that one person cannot fulfil all the needs of another when we are all of a unique disposition: some from Mars, others from Venus and all those in between.

Amélie and Bernadette, close friends of both Roisin and Arrabella, portrayed in the Marbella beach photo, entwined together in a playful hug look so free and familiar. Roisin remembers it being so heartwarming to see two very different women, with opposite characters and views, bonding. Amélie, always wearing her sexy red lipstick, her talons painted black, and her shiny black bob haircut swishing from side to side as she walks, has the touch and look of a black panther searching for her next kill. She is true to her Frenchness, a little opinionated, a few pointy edges and a strong sense of 'up with the workers'. She gives no quarter. She masks her vulnerabilities well.

Bernadette, on the other hand, is a true-blue Conservative, a solicitor in family law. Right and wrong is clear as day. She is practical and methodical, and ends her day with a Bible reading, as all good Catholic girls should.

Her auburn curly hair is usually under control, always ready for work. She is pretty in a natural way, not blingy. Occasionally she lets herself go and has a drink or two and then the true Irish lass comes bursting forth. Roisin reflects on that weekend and how all the ladies put their differences and worries aside and let go of the negative and just chilled, enjoying who they all were, women in need of downtime.

Roisin looks assiduously at the photo, at herself tucked in cosily between Kenise and Vivi, their arms linked over each other. She was where she wanted to be. She remembers the feeling of strength and empowerment shared between them; she hoped it would last forever. Vivi started her working life as a model and went on to marry a Greek shipping billionaire, one who conveniently died of a stroke after five years of marriage. She adores her girlfriends and luuurrves her men … she is a femme fatale and works it, with no time spared on guilt or commitment.

Her escapades take place in her London Mayfair house, her beach house in Saint-Tropez, numerous family homes in the Greek islands, a fashionable apartment in Milan and a chalet in Gstaad. She has a floor-to-ceiling brass pole in each dwelling as a showpiece for libertine private parties and smoochy liaisons and for exercise, so she says. Arrabella is one of her oldest besties.

Vivi usually has a few boyfriends to call on whenever she feels the need. Lawrence Willard, a lawyer and a recently acquired and most dynamic conquest, drops everything at her insistent demand. With a full head of strawberry blond floppy hair, youthful posh-boy banter and intellect, and a fervent desire to enhance his six-pack and harden his guns through lengthy sex marathons, he is topping her list right now. Vivi's tastes are varied. She has been known to venture off-piste, taking in locations fraught with danger. Roisin has noticed she has been overtly flirtatious with Leo Smyth of late. He is one such risk, as he is the husband of her dear friend Amélie.

Roisin is impressed by everything about Vivi. She would like to taste the freedom in her head, the selfishness that gets her everything she desires, the way she cuts through life, guilt- and worry-free. She has the power and money to be who and what she wants and manages to lure doting lovers and friends who want a piece of her spirited and big-hearted generous personality. Roisin is in awe of Vivi, but knows if Vivi set her sights on James, she could not compete and if Vivi offered herself to him, he could not resist the pleasure of her.

Kenise is a gem. Her father, Omario, was born in Jamaica, but lived most of his life in London, and he became a well-known drummer after playing on the *Dave Allen at Large* show from 1971 until 1986. He met Charlotte, Kenise's mother – a dancer from Buckinghamshire – on the show. Kenise inherited her father's gutsy, cheeky cockney spirit and humour, and her mother's beauty, home counties accent and dexterous social skills. Kenise is Roisin's university buddy and trusted confidante. They have a special bond forged through shared times of adversity and long-standing mutual respect. Roisin has always said that if she were ever shipwrecked on a desert island, she would want Kenise to be her Woman Friday, as she would hunt for food, build a boat, climb a mountain, stay positive, laugh and cry and charm the cannibals, convincing them we are more useful to them alive.

They also worked together in a private physiotherapy practice for women's health, which is where Kenise met her gorgeous gynaecologist boyfriend, Theodore Templer, while they were both tucked in between a pair of well-groomed pins, exploring the complexities of clitorodynia. Kenise has two daughters, Maya and Gracie, from a previous relationship. She has always been very protective of her girls, and bringing a man into their lives is a big issue for her. Theodore has been waiting eight years for Kenise to accept his proposal of marriage, but she has always worked hard to hide her pessimism that his love, like all love, is short-lived and when the day comes that it ends, it will hurt so much more if she has given her all to him. She is afraid to trust she is enough.

Roisin takes herself back to 4 June and the week she spent with her girlfriends in Marbella celebrating Arabella's birthday, in what they termed 'the hen house'. She remembers it as a time when she fought hard to enjoy every moment with the friends she loves, despite having found out that her husband had been unfaithful a few days before and that her life would soon implode. The uninterrupted view of blue and white frothy rolling waves caressing back and forth over groomed golden sand was heavenly. The fully open sliding glass doors along the full length of the beach side of the house welcomed in the warm breeze and the smells of the ocean, setting the scene for the playful bikini-clad ladies to let their inhibitions overflow, along with the Bollinger.

'OK, ladies,' Arrabella said, standing up proudly in her skimpy, barely there, multi-coloured, retro-design bikini, raising her glass, 'here's to ladies only, letting it all hang out, wobbly boobs, big bottoms and growing old disgracefully! Chin, chin, down the hatch in one.'

Roisin stood to attention. 'Says she with the washboard tum and obedient tits. How do I tame these nunga-nungas?' she hollered like a fish wife, bouncing her already-escaping breasts up and down vigorously with both hands, followed by a chorus of laughter, and a bent-over Kenise twerking frantically with the slightest flash of a shiny cerise strip of thong peeking out from the crack of her voluptuous booty with each push upwards towards the ceiling.

'Now, now, ladies, keep it dignified! One must not let oneself slip into mayhem and debauchery so quickly,' proclaimed Bernadette, preaching like the pontiff himself, always the voice of reason, while slugging back a full flute of fizz and then blowing a kiss to the baying crowd.

'Here, here, and another bolly for the lady in the leopard-design two-piece and sexy silk kimono,' shouted Amélie in an exaggerated French accent. Bernadette took a bow. Vivi, usually the first to play her hand, took the floor.

'If you lot were a group of guys, we would all be sucking and fucking before the sun went down. There is a whole party out there just begging for us. Put your knitting away, put your silky knickers on, or better still no knickers, and let's hit the bars and find the bangers.'

'Vivi,' screamed Arrabella, shaking her head, 'it's not

that kind of party. Stay off the booze, you sex nymph.'

Roisin spoke up, clinking Vivi's glass with her own, 'I'm with Vivi. Her kind of party sounds like just what I need right now.'

'Oooh la la, moi aussi,' Amélie confirmed, showing off her red-hot bikini-bod, sexy wiggle and pout.

'Tomorrow night we play,' said Vivi with devilish intent. Polly entered the living room, waving her hands in the air, having only just arrived at the house. 'I'm in,' she declared, laughing, having no idea as to what she was saying yes to.

'Anyone for a Neuhaus chocolate,' Bernadette piped up, attempting to dissuade further interest in Viv's lifestyle choices.

Roisin made a point of waiting until Vivi was alone. There were things that she might know that Roisin needed to know. Very soon, Vivi was lying on the sunbed by the pool, topless. Roisin couldn't tell if her eyes were open or closed due to her wearing dark sunglasses. Roisin hovered around her, looking for signs that she was not asleep. Roisin took in her almost nakedness. 'God, she is so fit,' she thought, while admiring her gladiatorial, athletic, tanned body stretched over the flattened sunbed. 'She is a work of art.'

Vivi's right arm was raised, her hand clasped into a fist, sitting in the nape of her neck. Her head was facing the opposite direction. Roisin admired the perfection and magnificence of her breasts, perusing every curve and her large erect nipples. 'She looks like a woman in the throes of an orgasm,' Roisin imagined, wishing she could feel what, and how, Vivi felt for just one week. 'What pleasures are on your mind right now, Vivi?' she wondered. 'I may be a willing student if you and I were to come to a place where only delectation mattered.' Roisin's fantasy came to a stop at the sound of Vivi's voice.

'Do you like what you see, Roisin?' she said in a direct manner.

Roisin, taken back at having been caught leching over her friend's exposed body, hesitated with her answer. 'How could I not like what I see? You are an impressive woman in every way.' Roisin couldn't believe she had said that out loud – now Vivi would know she was turned on. 'There is something I need to ask you, Vivi, about your ex, Roland.' Roisin trod tentatively, knowing Vivi's affair with Roland had ended very badly, with each of them wanting to kill the other.

'Oh, that complete knob. Tell me he has died from pussy asphyxiation, and I will be one happy woman.'

'Erm, no, unfortunately not, but I think he has been providing Russian escort girls for James, who told me he is in London working with Roland on a property development site,' Roisin blurted out, relieved to tell someone.

Vivi might have been wild and a law unto herself, but she was loyal to Roisin and would want to support her if James had been unfaithful. 'Roland had to ditch the sex work as part of his moving-in deal with his super-wealthy Korean heiress girlfriend Bong-cha. Her daddy threatened to stop her mega allowance unless he cleaned up his act, but rumour has it, he stepped back from front-line operations and continues to control finances. He still calls the shots, but now he hides in the shadows. If her daddy knew what debauchery Roland and his little girl get up to on the sex scene with rich fuckers, Roland would disappear.'

'Does Milaya Investments mean anything to you, Vivi?' Roisin asked, suspecting she already knew the answer.

'It's a Russian term, meaning "love transactions", and the name of Mr Roland Reeves' private investment company – very lucrative from what I hear,' Vivi stated serenely, while taking hold of Roisin's face gently in both hands, planting a lingering kiss on her lips. 'I'm here always if you need me,' Vivi whispered, her cheek pressed against Roisin's. 'Just call.' Roisin did not move, not even a blink of the eye. She stood up and nodded a yes. They had had a moment.

That evening, between the fresh food being prepared and enjoyed, and the drip, drip of alcohol consumed amid the games and laughter, Vivi and Roisin shared knowing glances. Roisin drank more than she should have done. Right now she needed to be a fun girlfriend, not a miserable and broken wife to a cheating husband. Roisin knew she was going to have to confront her failing marriage. Living in denial was something she could not do, but for now she wanted to be just Roisin and enjoy carefree moments with her girlfriends.

A perky Polly jumped on the sofa, shaking a pair of maracas. 'Ladies, ladies, I would like you all to share with everyone here your most favourite magical place or experience. The birthday girl must go first.' Arrabella rolled her eyes.

'OK ... not sure I want to share my most exciting experiences with you lot,' she said, sniggering, still rolling her eyes. 'OK, Barnaby and I, and our four gorgeous girls, who you all know very well, went to Soho Farmhouse last year for my birthday.' A loud, unruly whooping noise came from the hens. 'And,' Arrabella continued with rising excitement, her piercing blue cat-like eyes now wide open, engaging with her onlookers, 'David Beckham ... yes, Becks himself was standing a few feet away from me ... The man of my dreams,' she said, disclosing her delight. 'I said to my girls, "This may be my one chance to get close to him, maybe even speak to him ... I would be happy just to choke on his aftershave." All four of my girls looked so hot in their slinky, skimpy dresses, that I told them to go and distract him and his bodyguard, while I put myself in position ... and they did. Well, before I could congratulate myself, Becks suddenly turned around and stepped forward, clearly not expecting anyone to be standing so close behind him. He stood on my Jimmy Choos ... and ... if it wasn't for him putting his strong arm around my waist and pulling me towards him, I would have landed flat on my back. "Good job I saved you," he said, smiling. Honestly, I was so close I could taste his drink spraying off his tongue, and my girls caught it all on their phones. They often remind me of the day I stalked and groped David Beckham.'

'Three cheers for Becks and Arrabella!' Vivi shouted, starting off a chorus. Roisin was relieved to be distracted by the laughter around her.

A very excited Polly quickly jumped in on the last hip, hip, hooray. 'Me next,' she insisted, flicking her strawberry-blonde feathered fringe away from her eyes. She captured her audience with poise and an unblinking wide-eyed gaze over the room. Roisin knows Polly is a pro at falling into character and telling a story with flair and panache, and listened attentively to her story, a much-needed interruption from thinking about James. 'It was turning to dusk,' she began her recital, with all the spectacle of *A Midsummer Night's Dream*, 'with the heat of the sun giving out her last. I was shimmying through the trees, heading towards the gently rolling waves when I came across a nestled sandy enclave. In the centre, glowing hot embers and snaking ribbons of smoke rose from a thrown-together fire, making their way to the darkening skies. I joined a group squatting around the fire smoking ganja and drinking rum. I noticed there was a bamboo limbo game set up between two palm trees. I sauntered through the camp like I owned the place, demanding we have an impromptu limbo competition ... and we did. I was positively sexy in my short, flowery cotton dress and bare feet ... and, let's not forget, ladies, a damn sexy, flexy twenty-one-year-old. It was epic!' Polly shrieked with delight. 'I won, and this big gorgeous black guy threw me over his shoulder and carried me off at speed down to the ocean's edge and—' Polly gasped.

'And?' shouted Roisin. 'You could have skipped all the theatre and palaver and got down to the most memorable bit of the story – the amazing shag on the beach with the biggest wanger you have ever seen in your life.'

The air filled with the sound of side-splitting cackling from the hens. 'Erm, erm ... it was poetry,' insisted Polly, very loudly with a naughty grin on her face, 'not shagging.'

Polly came and sat next to Roisin, remembering her friend was still grieving the loss of her stepson, Noah. Roisin gave her a hug, reassuring her that this fun was just what she needed right now, but her mind was on talking to Vivi. She needed more information in case James spun her a yarn and Vivi might be able to help.

'You can tell me the details of your "poetry" later, Polly,' Kenise shouted across the room. Sprawled out like Cleopatra on a cream chaise longue, pina colada in hand, she decided to speak up, and speak her mind. 'My most fabulous and mind-blowing experience is yet to come.' She paused, busy moving away stuff and fruit sticking out of her glass with her fingers. She took a long slow sip of her cocktail, while the ladies remained still and quiet, patiently waiting for her to rise out from her fruit salad and finish her speech. 'I'm going to marry my handsome Theodore Templer, my gorgeous, smart gynaecologist.'

'When is the wedding?' Bernadette asked. 'I do love a wedding.'

'The next time he asks me to marry him, I'm going to say yes. After eight years together, I'm finally ready to surrender to him. I realise I now want to be his wife, Mrs Kenise Templer,' she said, raising her empty glass, content with her declaration and its certainty.

'Oh, it's not a done deal then, Kenise?' Arrabella pointed out. 'It will definitely change how I see the handsome Theodore during my next appointment if I see a flash of wedding ring before his head descends down into my fandango. I never know what's best, a Brazilian, or a smart runway so he can land successfully. A gynaecologist should never be that good-looking,' she said with a wry smile.

'My Theo,' Kenise piped up, 'has had his head in so many monster minges, he is grateful for my perfect au naturel self.

He calls mine "his purring panther".'

'He hasn't met my tiger,' Vivi added. 'Where does he practice? I could do with a once-over.' Kenise threw Vivi a look, one which said, 'over my dead body bitch.' Roisin jumped in, taking advantage of the awkward pause to change the subject. All this innuendo around fancying another woman's love and talk of happy weddings was getting to her. It no longer felt like fun.

'One of my standout moments must be my epic performance on the ski slopes, keeping up with the mighty force that is Arrabella, head-to-head from the top of a challenging blue run, Le Creux in Les Trois Vallees, to the end of the run and finishing at Courchevel for an all-night apres-ski celebration. I was no longer her pupil.' Arrabella, standing by the kitchen island, poured herself a glass of water while listening to the story and began nodding her head.

'It's true. She was on my heels all the way, though she forgot to tell you it took her ten years, and half a bottle of XO brandy to keep up with me.' Roisin, feeling very emotional, fought back a tear. She knew this was true, but it was undoubtedly her most perfect and precious memory, particularly now that her knee replacement had put paid to her ever having that level of control, speed and confidence again.

'Only Vivi left,' shouted Arrabella. 'Come on, your whole life has been a playground.' Vivi took centre stage, swaggered a little and cleared her throat.

'Mmm … so many to choose from. I was in Milan with Lawrence, the lawyer. We were stood outside the Duomo in Milan, the third-largest cathedral in the world and we decided to do the rooftop tour.'

'Oh, I have always wanted to do that tour,' interrupted Bernadette. 'It's so on my list of exciting things to see. Carry on, Vivi.'

'So, we climbed the stairs and arrived at the top to the most magical view of Milan. It was breathtaking. The magnificent architectural pillars, the scary gargoyles, all beautiful shades of white and soft pinks, having recently been renovated. It was hot, so hot on that roof ... and Lawrence looked so hot in his khaki shorts and open-neck linen shirt.' Roisin listened with jealousy in her heart. She knew what was coming – the kind of sex she remembers having with James on their first date in the Chesterfield hotel.

'I grabbed Lawrence by the scruff of his collar with both hands and shoved him in a corner behind an ugly gargoyle, hidden out of view, and snogged his face off. Sensing a little reluctance, I said hello to big boy, coaxing him out to play. We fucked furiously. It was the most thrilling, frightening two minutes of my life. I swear the grimacing, then laughing gargoyle in front of me was the Devil himself getting off on my orgasm, enjoying the defilement of the house of the opposition. Everything moved in that two minutes. I did feel a pang of remorse as we hotfooted it down the stairs. I thought we would be struck down by the Almighty before we reached the bottom door, the door that represents the Joy and Sorrow of the Virgin Mary. I now know how she feels,' Vivi said, finishing her story to a shocked and silent audience.

'Well, moving on,' Arrabella remarked, 'Vivi won't be getting old and sensible anytime soon, anyone for tea?' she asked, trying to infuse a little dignity among the hens ... the room remained silent.

'When I am old and in a twelve-foot by twelve-foot care-home room,' Roisin suddenly boomed, 'ok, older and just about clinging on to my faculties, I will be clutching on to my false teeth, lipstick and vibrator with unbecoming tenacity. I never want to succumb to bingo or playing bean bag games.'

Arrabella shouted across from the kitchen sink with gusto, 'Hope to God I'm not in the next room, staring up at the ceiling, not able to sleep, because of your buzzing all night long, you dirty bitch.'

'I do hope I stay rich and posh, darlings. I could not do poor,' Arrabella said, wincing at the thought.

Kenise, with her old wise head, intervened. 'There are diffcrent types of posh, ladies. Please let's stick to what we do best: sophisticated, perfectly prim and pruned. Only a subtle hint of Hermes and Tiffany on show, to avoid raping and pillaging, and please do fuck the gardener only when the daddy of the house is doing long haul.' A loud raucous cheer erupted, and a clink of champagne glasses filled the room. Bernadette, still trying to process the act of violation on the roof of the cathedral, sought out Roisin for solace.

'She's made that up. Surely that can't be true.'

'Yeah, she likes to shock. Even Vivi wouldn't do that.' Roisin walked away, believing she had just told a lie.

. . .

As the long weekend rolled by, the hens spent sunny days sunbathing and talking, walking on the beachfront and talking, shopping and talking, eating, drinking one too many and talking, endlessly putting the world to rights. Roisin felt something bigger was taking place. The conversations that she was part of all came from the same place: a woman's need to be with women. As they got older, this need seemed to get greater and hold more value in their daily lives. The reliance on men weakened with age and it was girlfriends who offered understanding and a supporting shoulder. Roisin had never known this wonder, passed down through mothers and aunties. Her instinct had always been to turn to a man, but men, she had learnt, have other motives.

She listened to the constant gabbling about everything and anything, and found it reassuring and comforting and no longer an irritant. No friendship was harmed in the hen house. Even Bernadette and Vivi agreed that when their time was up, they would meet and wish each other luck before stepping on the stairway to heaven or hell – both very sure of which route they would be taking. Polly, being Polly, sensed Roisin was hiding her feelings in alcohol-fuelled laughter and overindulgence. Roisin couldn't bring herself to tell her that soon she would have to confront James's infidelity and face the shit storm heading her way.

Bernadette, seeing the two of them huddled together, concerned and guessing the topic of conversation, spoke out.

'How is James coping now? Is it getting any easier, you know, losing Noah?' Roisin took a deep gulp ... Now that her mind was on also losing James, she couldn't go there, not now, not tonight.

7

MUMMY TWO

The present, Saturday, 10 a.m.

Roisin draws some comfort from sharing her worries with Polly, who is all about looking at the bigger picture and forgiveness. She hangs up the phone wanting to take that road and save her marriage. She heads upstairs to her bedroom to continue with her journey through her memories, trying to work through her gut feeling that James, too, is another man, like Ian and Andreas, who is destructive for her. Or is he just a man who made a terrible mistake? She passes by Noah's room and her heart sinks as a wave of distress rushes through her, remembering that beautiful boy who was so desperately unhappy that he took his own life. Roisin always knew that at some point in her life, she wanted to become a mother.

It was always complicated for her, not straightforward. Fall in love, bang, bang, two kids later, a family. It was never that way and could never be that way. Not having a mother to look upon, to feel, from her breast to her view of life, was a curse. One which shrouded motherhood in mystery and left a gaping wound which festered through the years. An empty void, a blackness that gnawed away at femininity and the whole meaning of what it is to be female, to nurture and be a giver and provider of life. After the trauma of the family life she had known, it became natural to crave solitude. Families argue, fight and destroy each other. Escaping that was about survival and not just a lifestyle choice.

Roisin wanted and searched for love for many years in the wrong places, while her womb lay empty and useless, and her heart hardened, and the belief that she deserved or would ever receive true love and happiness was never an expectation. Her one chance, when her mind and body demanded motherhood, raging through her like a firestorm, came all too late and ended in death and grief. She did not know what it was she was going to miss, until it was too late. Being Mummy Two was a role she embraced. She accepted she was naive as to the right actions and decisions to take, but after having '*a wicked stepmother*' she also felt she knew of the things she should not do and be.

For the first months of their relationship, Roisin was under the radar, James's every-other-weekend playmate, separate from the complications and challenges he was facing in his real life. For Roisin, staying in the shadows meant the rush of excitement was thrilling and the need to be together was always soaring at its peak. The last thing they both wanted at this time was suffocating moments of silence and dependency. Meeting his children was a bit of an accident.

James mostly worked from home and offered to look after Twiglet when Roisin was working long hours and when the lady next door went on holiday. On one such day, she finished work earlier than expected. It was a day when Ethan and Noah were usually with their mother at her house, so when she rang the bell at James's, she was surprised to see a blond-haired, handsome young man opening the door, and Twiglet running past him then jumping excitedly up her legs.

'Hello,' Roisin said, not sure of what she should say next. 'Are you Ethan or Noah?' she asked as Twiglet became impatient for her attention.

'This is Noah,' James said, suddenly appearing in the doorway, holding Blade back by his collar. 'This is Roisin, Twiglet's mummy. Do you think we should ask her to come in for a cup of tea, Noah?' James said looking at Noah for a response.

'Yup,' Noah said, scurrying under his dad's arm and back into the house.

Roisin, looking very surprised, stood still with a contented Twiglet in her arms, mouthing the word 'sorry'. James just looked at Roisin with a sort of smile on his face which said, 'let's give it a go', while beckoning her in. James had told her so much about his boys over the previous six months and many stories about the wonderful holidays they had enjoyed as a family. But up until this moment, Ethan and Noah had not known that she existed. The boys were engrossed in playing the game Roblox on their computers. Her presence had little, if any, impact. Roisin avoided touching James in any way in front of his boys and just enjoyed watching him being dad, while she nursed a hot cup of tea.

Both boys said hello and goodbye, and Ethan picked up Twiglet and placed her in Roisin's arms when she left. James saw that as a success.

After many more cups of tea together, with Twiglet in tow, it was Ethan who, during their first evening meal together at James's house, cheekily asked, while his younger brother was giggling, 'Are you Dad's girlfriend?'

James looked straight at Roisin, reached over and grasped hold of her hand and said, 'Yes, she is.' In that moment, for Roisin, time stood still. She sat next to a man whom she loved, but dared not speak the words to; she sat opposite two young boys whom she liked, and who she hoped would like her; and Twiglet and Blade, who were way ahead of all of them, lying snuggled into each other on the settee like they had known each other for years.

This was the closest she had ever been to something that felt like her family. Roisin thought James oblivious to the various emotions running amok through her mind while she sat opposite his sons, enjoying what for him was a normal, casual evening, eating a meal of sausage, mash and beans. And why would he have been aware of her need to analyse her place within his family. They hadn't been dating long and he certainly wasn't thinking long term. But Roisin was very much aware of the joy, the fun, the growing attachment to … then having to come to terms with the heartache of what may have been, when he moved on to another love.

Four months later she was sat at the same table feeling very different. She had moved in with James on his suggestion after a particularly romantic evening spent at the Le Gavroche, where they met Michel Roux Jr who presented her with a red rose, and when James told her he loved her very much. She rented out her beloved Victorian terrace and moved to live with James in his five-bedroom country house in Barston village.

His wife Talia remained in the palatial marital home, initially taking on the lion's share of their sons' care. Talia had requested a face-to-face meeting with the woman who would be spending time with her boys. Everything about the first time Roisin met Talia is engraved on her memory. It was a weekend when the boys were with James at his house. Talia arrived in a blacked-out Range Rover and exited with the confidence of a gangster's moll. She was imposing and impressive with her long black hair swishing around her shoulders as she walked to the front door.

She wore a black trouser suit with a crisp white openneck shirt collar. It was a real power look and had the desired effect. Roisin feeling completely out-gunned in the dress and swagger department, felt like shrinking away in her fluffy slippers and cream polo-neck jumper. She stood nervously behind a kitchen chair, gripping onto its back, not quite knowing what to do with her hands, as she watched Talia walk closer to her with an unflinching gaze.

'So, you're Roisin. The boys tell me you are a leg rubber, and I gather you have been rubbing my husband's leg for five years?'

Her words, spoken with delivery as sharp as a Japanese yanagiba sashimi knife, and a generous helping of cynicism, indicated that she already knew the answer to her question. Ethan and Noah, hearing their mother's voice, rushed over to her, severing the awkwardness.

'Mummy, did you bring the cheesy sticks and gummies?' Ethan pleaded. 'You promised …'

'No, sweetie. They're at home,' she replied in a softer Californian coastal urban accent. After a twenty-minute hard-and-fast interrogation, one that felt like it lasted ninety minutes, Talia established that they were very much her boys and Roisin should not overrule her, try to change them or lay a hand on them. She made it clear that Roisin should follow her direction regarding their needs always. This was a whole new experience for Roisin and, having no children of her own, it felt like a minefield.

'Now you're living with James – you are living with James, right? I want your contact details,' Talia said, her tone turning austere, as she swung her head towards her husband. 'Could you not have waited until the ink was dry on the divorce papers?' James did his best to stay silent and avoid even the slightest contribution to the process of setting the ground rules, leaving Roisin to take the hit. 'And make sure they clean their teeth morning and night,' Talia said as her parting directive.

Roisin felt a nurturing love developing for the boys as she spent more time with them. She often recalls the sweet, loving moments, like the time when Noah snuggled into her while trying to hide from the scary hanging cobwebs and the monsters in the spooky darkness of the ghost train, and when Ethan, always playful and affectionate, would throw his arm across her for a cuddle while watching a film. She loved being their friend, a playmate, and James made it clear that's how he wanted to keep it.

Considering the disruption his children were dealing with, he alone wanted to deal with boundaries and behaviour, which made perfect sense in the early days. He wanted their time with him to be all about fun, and Roisin would always cherish those times. On the flip side, it took four years for James and Talia to divorce. Their battle lines became a warren of tunnels, black holes and never-ending tit for tat with neither wanting to concede to the other. And both of them lost a stack of money while sinking in their respective ground. Talia wanted to return to California with her children, so a custody battle ensued. The boys spent four years going back and forth from one house to the other, controlling the narrative, pitting their parents against one another in order to gain the most advantageous position. They changed from being two rather cute boys into mini manipulative dictators.

They made the rules, they stopped going to school, they played computer games all day and every day, they had au pairs and insisted that their life of doing only what they wanted and being waited on continued. For Roisin, it was tragic viewing. She tried her best to keep out of the firing line, suggesting the adults in the room slug it out between themselves at arranged times when she was out of the house. She loved James, but she knew Talia had a right to fight too. She watched as they both became overwhelmed and desperate in their quest to win their war. In the end, both boys made the decision for themselves, and chose to live with their dad. Roisin reckoned it was doing all the fun boy stuff that sealed the deal. But she was pleased for herself too. They might not have been her children, but she now had the family she had longed for. Talia returned to her family in California, bought a beautiful house, fell in love and returned to her previous line of work as an interior design consultant.

Roisin, in the peacefulness of her bedroom, with her photos spread all around her, reflects on those first four years: they were both bitter and sweet. How she became used to the status quo of having to smooth over in her mind the jagged edges, the falling apart of their family, the cutting words batted between James and Talia due to stressful disagreements dredged up and used as evidence to fortify their respective divorce and custody demands. It was, for Roisin too, a tearing down of the boundaries that keep kindness, thoughtfulness and logic at the forefront of every decision. A time when what you have and what you are bleeds painfully out, despite the endless sticking plasters. It takes a righteous mindset, or a stubborn stance, to land a thousand bloody blows and demonise your opponent, especially someone you had promised to love 'until death do us part'. In some way, Roisin accepted the battle played out before her.

Neither James nor Talia wanted to be together, they were in their death throes, just as she had once been with Andreas. Four people who were in the wrong place at the wrong time and could not communicate.

In the end, Talia left her sons, even though they were hurting as a result of the prolonged disruption in their lives. Noah was never able to express his feelings, and him choosing to live with his dad came as a shock. Maybe Talia needed to find herself again. Roisin feels her staying would not have changed the boys. Both parents would have never agreed, and their war would have rolled on.

The damage was done and the consequences for their young hearts and minds mapped out a tangled future. Ethan, both a pig and a pearl, at the age of seventeen was handsome, gregarious, smart and wildly funny. His sexuality was very much a mystery. 'Yo! I ain't no maid' and 'Only wagyu will do' were common phrases he would spout while strutting through the kitchen, avoiding domestic chores and turning down a perfectly cooked slab of steak. Unlike Ethan, Noah noticed the au pairs. Initially he was sweet, kind and laid-back, and he welcomed the opportunity to be mothered. He needed Roisin, but with time he withdrew and sank into a dark depression. He would never again lift himself up to a better place. James, and now Roisin, had a challenge on their hands. During those early teenage years, there were many times when Roisin saw Talia as having dodged a bullet, one any mother who is missing the joy her children can also bring, may never recognise. If either Roisin or Talia thought for one moment that there was a risk that Noah's life could be so cruelly cut short, their own decisions and direction may have looked very different.

James fought hard over the years to instil the old-fashioned values that he had been brought up with, a solid education, a strong work ethic, good manners, and a desire for more than childish pursuits. He was an older dad, who wanted a less turbulent journey, and his efforts often fell on deaf ears. It was too late. They were sixteen and seventeen, strong willed, wayward, ruined by the wealth they had access to, all their needs easily met. The boys squandered their days in idle pursuits and meaningless distractions.

Their permanent state of bodily languor was an irritant to Roisin. And for James, it was a burden that lay heavy on his heart – a rich man's curse, that neither of his sons had the business acumen, or the desire to work as hard as he had. Why would they opt for working long hours, commitment and facing the difficult decisions that needed to be made, when they could have all the luxury without a day's work? Roisin spent years trying to present how people less fortunate live, the poverty, the starving, the vulnerable ... but they could not see it, or feel it. It felt like a lost cause.

In their early twenties, they finally listened to their dad, took the bait, worked for him and became mostly independent. But without the fire in their bellies, the years went by and they missed out on the bigger picture and the things that make life rich and varied, a girlfriend, or boyfriend, a lover, a desire to leave your bedroom, and put down tracks with friends, see the world and follow their own dreams, and eventually leave home. James, Roisin and Talia waited patiently, hoping soon there would come a day, a lightbulb moment. They had everything, and yet happiness eluded them ... and then came the pandemic.

8

FROM DOOR TO DOOR

The present, Saturday, 11.15 a.m.

Roisin looks up at the kitchen clock. She notices how slowly time appears to go by when you are alone, with only your thoughts. She needs time to stop, to keep the heartache at bay at least until she feels strong enough to unpick her sham of a marriage and face the raging tempest she will stir once she challenges her husband. She has always admired James for his masterly competence in business and his prowess in the court room. She reminds herself of his long battle with Talia, a worthy and fierce opponent. He was astute and unwavering. Roisin knows she neither has the stomach nor the cunning to survive a duel. But her need for self-respect demands she does the right thing, and stands her ground.

Suddenly the intercom rings, interrupting her melancholy, alerting her to the presence of a delivery van at the gate. She is hoping it is her favourite Belgian chocolates – she could do with a sweet distraction. Alone in the house, she decides to collect the box through the parcel hatch. Jax and Coco charge by her side up to the gate, looking and sounding menacing and ready to bite. Returning to the house, Roisin finds herself facing her own front door, standing still, frozen in a moment in time. As she peruses the lines and dimensions of the bespoke and skilfully crafted solid oak door, her hand sweeps over the ornate brass centrepiece, recalling the many front doors from her past. None were as impressive or exuded such gravity and pre-eminence, but each came with peering faces and hands that would lead Roisin and her beleaguered siblings to a new stay, a place to eat, another family to share.

The many opening and closing doors, forgotten faces, comforting hands – and a few that left a repugnant mark – were now only fleeting memories. Cajoling and competing for legitimacy as proof of experiences once lived, they were therefore worthy of archiving and dredging out at any time of despair and self-loathing. Looking back on her life, Roisin sees it as a labyrinth of winding roads she had to choose from, pathways to find, and meandering rivers to roll upon. She truly believes that where you start from and the ground in which you grow sets your roadmap, and that only the gift of chance can bring happiness.

Age four, Roisin was living at 40 Ansty Lane, Leicester, where she enjoyed the closeness of attentive, maternal and paternal love. She remembers riding on her favourite squeaky blue bus around the big circle of summer grass, overlooked by what she saw as the many admiring smiling faces of pretty flowers. Roisin knows she was happy with Mr and Mrs Beck, her foster parents, and their very tall teenage son, Adam. She was the only other child living with them and cannot remember even being aware that she had a brother and sister living in care elsewhere. The black-and-white photos, showing her big smiles while feeding the ducks in Abbey Park and playing in her Wendy house in the garden, tell her she was loved. She doesn't remember leaving; she just remembers arriving at the next house to collect her brother and sister who she did not know, to move elsewhere together.

Roisin can still recall the sudden screeching of the rusty metal gate as it opened, interrupting the noise of passing cars, and the choking engine fumes. She tightly held the hand of Miss June Dean, her social worker, as she was ushered up the steep concrete steps to the place she was told was Darra's and Orla's house. At the age of seven she was about to be reunited with her brother and sister. Dressed in a flowery dress, white ankle socks and shiny black shoes, holding her pink satchel bag containing all her drawing materials, she stood in front of the dirty grey door with its paint peeling off and next to the broken toys strewn on the path. The tiny, grassed area was overgrown, and she could hear a lot of crying and commotion coming from the other side of the door.

The door to the Leicester city terrace house was opened by a large woman with a screaming toddler straddling her hip.

'Come on in,' she said, without any niceties. The house was chaotic, with noisy children running up and down the hallway and in and out of the living room. The smells were sickly and unpleasant. 'They're over there,' the woman pointed, shoving a dummy in the youngster's mouth. Darra and Orla, who had been separated from their big sister due to no foster parent wanting three children, sat silent, with their arms entwined. They seemed lost among the cries and wants of the other demanding toddlers. They looked unwashed, with greasy hair, and wore stained and ill-fitting clothes.

Roisin, feeling upset at being in this situation, pulled herself closer to Miss June Dean, grasping her hand a little tighter. The three children were then directed into the back seat of the car. Roisin moved to the furthest point she could, leaning into the car door while Darra and Orla huddled together, clinging on to one another for familiarity and affection. The children sat staring at each other throughout the journey to a farmhouse in Great Glen. When they arrived, they saw a big tyre hanging from a rope attached to a high branch of a tree in the garden and heard fearsome barking coming from around the back of the house. A chubby bald man, wearing a baggy check shirt, jeans and muddy boots, opened the door.

Once inside, the smells were different from the last house – the stench of dogs and the burning smell from a coal fire in the main room. Three older children were sitting on the floor by the fire, two girls and a boy, all with unexcited and distant expressions. They watched Roisin and her siblings walk into the living room and sit down on a leather settee. Roisin felt her stomach tightening. This house was nothing like Mr and Mrs Beck's house. It felt eerie, old and austere.

The older children, whose home it was, never accepted the presence of Roisin, Darra and Orla. They were cruel and hit out whenever their parents were out of sight. Mr and Mrs Lumley were strict, and they used their Alsatian dogs, most of them kept outside in a huge pen, to threaten the children.

'You behave, do as you're told, or you will spend the night in with the dogs,' the foster parents would say, time and time again. One time, Roisin was squatting down in the corner of the living room reading a schoolbook, when she suddenly saw Darra trapped in a stranglehold by Mr Lumley, trying to wriggle himself free.

'You little rag,' he growled, 'I told you not to run around. You're for the dogs,' he shouted, charging towards the back door in nothing but a stained pair of baggy grey Y-fronts.

Roisin leapt up, dropping her book on the floor, screaming, 'No ... no,' and running after them at speed, followed closely by Orla. Mr Lumley dangled Darra over the dog compound, his legs flailing, crying for his life. Orla, too, grabbing onto Roisin, started to squeal. 'Shuuush, Orla, shush,' Roisin said sharply, startling her. 'Please, please!' Roisin implored. 'I promise he will be a good boy from now on. I promise.'

'He'd better,' Mr Lumley said, throwing Darra to the ground.

Everyone told Orla to shush every time she cried. She grew more silent with each day, until no one saw her. Roisin noticed that all her nice clothes and toys now belonged to the other girls. After a few weeks, she looked grubby, her red hair unwashed and in knots.

Orla stayed silent, afraid and tearful, and Darra was constantly trying to thwart the older boy's bullying and keep out of the way of the bad-tempered Mr Lumley. She found her solace in reading books from school and drawing. It was a purely financial arrangement; the three strangers were not wanted. They lived at the farmhouse in Great Glen for a year. It was a terrible year.

Roisin remembers the day they were taken to the kindly Mrs Muggleton and her white chocolate-box cottage opposite the village church in Husbands Bosworth. They were together and happy. It was a good day, a summer's day. The air was filled with the smell of freshly cut grass and there were flowers everywhere, outside and inside the house.

Mrs Muggleton placed a plate of chocolate cookies on a round table in the kitchen.

'All for us?' Darra asked in disbelief, as she smiled and ushered the children towards the table. She had the softest, kindest voice and golden curls that fell onto her cheeks every time she leant down to talk to the children. Roisin was so tempted to ping those curls and see how high they bounced. Every Sunday afternoon at four o'clock, they would all sit together and snuggle on the comfy sofas next to the coal fire, eat chocolate buttons covered with a thousand colourful candy sprinkles and watch *The Adventures of Black Beauty* on the TV. Roisin could see the front door to the church opposite from her bedroom window. She was nosy and loved to watch the comings and goings.

She joined the Sunday school choir where she developed a love of singing in the echoey chambers of the church, but she never came to appreciate the bell ringing early every Sunday morning when she wanted to sleep. Everyone who went to the church opposite, the blacksmith next door, the farmer who owned the fields and lake at the back of the white cottage, and the corner-shop lady, all came to know Roisin, Darra and Orla. They lived in the village of Husbands Bosworth for three years. Three years of adventure and happiness with Grandma Muggleton ... only then to be snatched away by social services.

Their father had arranged for them to be collected and delivered to him and his girlfriend, the woman they would come to know as Eileen. Seamus and Eileen stood leaning over the black metal balcony on the second floor of a concrete housing block in the area known as Highfields and for its flourishing red-light district. They waited while the children ascended the two flights of stairs. Dragging a heavy school bag over the grubby steps, Roisin looked at the graffiti on the bleak grey walls that were cold to the touch. There was an unpleasant smell in these corridors, unfamiliar and unlike that of the grass and flowers in the garden at Mrs Muggleton's cottage. Roisin felt sick with worry. Darra and Orla were too young to imagine what might lie before them.

9

MOTHER

The present, Saturday, 12.30 p.m.

Her absence takes away almost everything, and what's missing is hard to find.

Among all the photos strewn on the bed, Roisin notices a bunch of envelopes of different sizes tied together by a piece of string. She knows one of those letters is handwritten by her mother and addressed to Darra. He could not bring himself to meet her face to face. He has never been able to deal with the rejection and knowing she went on to have three more children who she cared for so soon after leaving her first three. It was the final death blow. For Darra, becoming a father meant he could never forgive her. Having shared the same hurt and bitterness, Roisin thought he had made the right decision. He read the letter once and handed it to Roisin.

'What can I do with this?' he said, placing the letter in her hand, shaking his head from side to side, unable to find the words to express his feelings.

Roisin still remembers many of her mother's heartfelt written words, her explanation for why she abandoned her vulnerable babies to the fate of a man she knew to be violent, choosing to think of only her own needs and future. Roisin considered it a rather weak plea that she had put forward in the hope her dumped children would have room for understanding her side of the story, from her point of view. Suddenly feeling the urge to read her mother's reasoning once again, Roisin reaches over to pick up the bundle, but then becomes distracted by the sight of a small blue envelope. Her heart skips a beat as she realises it has been years since she last looked at its contents: an image that holds so much importance for her and a poem that she felt fitting to write and place with it, before sealing its memory safely away.

The small black-and-white Polaroid-type photo with an image only an expectant parent would recognise, the hospital baby scan photo showing her the gift of life that would soon become the focus of her every day, and entwined in every aspect of her future, or so she thought. Roisin stares into the black hole, the nurturing space giving sanctuary to her longed-for baby, conceived through trial and deceit, rather than what she once hoped for, a strong and loving relationship. Roisin feels the tears roll down her face as she remembers the painful moment she was told her baby had died in the womb at three months old and with it her last hope and dream of becoming a mother. It was 2010; her relationship with Andreas was over. It died with her baby. She was consumed with loss and grief, and all she could think about was the life that she thought was ahead of her and that was now gone. She couldn't let go of the 'what if' and 'if only'. Her baby was there when she walked down the street and watched new mothers stopping to present their little one, their smiling faces as they settled their baby comfortably on their bosoms, bouncing their pride and joy to the sound of coos and gurgles.

Her child was there when she went past a playground, a nursery class, a school … anywhere young voices could be heard, screeching with joy or crying out. Her child was there when friends spoke of the milestones their children had achieved and the wonderful plans they were making for their futures. She saw every mother go from mother to grandmother and saw the love on their faces and listened to the joy in their voices. And she wished she had grown old with her offspring. Roisin never knew if her baby was a boy or girl. It didn't matter, she just wished they were here. Roisin turns to the folded blue notepaper, opens it and reads the poem she wrote to herself that spoke of her broken heart …

... And I Have Wished You Were Here

In the wee hours, there you suckle and thrive
Of you I see, and then much, much more
My breast put to its purpose and there you grow
The rhythm of heartbeat, your touch and smell I come to know
And in my sleeping hours and the brightness of day
I see you become, how you see me and how you play
In your needs and cries and your first steps of everything
A skip and a hop in the schoolyard,
A twirl in your hand of daisy and buttercup
your discovery of worlds real and fantasy
A kitchen table speaks of your imagination and years of play
And as you prepare to leave me,
with your head full of innocence and dreams
My fears for you play out every minute of every day
My questioning – did I miss something of you along the way
And God knew I had so little time to bear you
One chance, one gift of love and promise of life anew
And this was my life with each breath I would see
But you came and went, and a mother I was never to be.

Roisin, 2010

And, in that moment, Roisin is no longer interested in reading her own mother's imploration for forgiveness. Instead, she searches for the photo that she held in her hand when she was twelve years old, the one that changed everything. Roisin's mother, Anna Tweedy, a Yorkshire lass, aged sixteen was wholly unprepared for the next three years and three babies. She married the twenty-year-old Seamus in haste at the sight of her first bump. Soon after they wed, his volatile and controlling nature was unleashed and showed no bounds. Roisin and her siblings, born into poverty, lived mainly with their young mother in a bedsit off the Melton Road in Leicester. Their father worked for Laing Construction, spending weeks at a time away from home.

Roisin thought there never was a more perfect bonny baby boy than Darra. Her younger brother was born in 1965. His delectable rosy cheeks and plump happy tummy must have melted seamlessly into his mother's breast. She would have tenderly swept aside his silky blond hair from his blushing brow, and cooed blissfully over her suckling babe, bonding ... watching those insistent warm brown eyes reflecting their pleasure and closing slowly on fulfilment. She gave life to not just one child but three, nurturing them to perfection, delivering them safely from the womb to her bosom.

Roisin knows now that she and her siblings were tethered to the equivalent of rotten driftwood. Both her parents were young and reckless. Her father's family lived in Northern Ireland, and her mother, whose own mother was preoccupied with her many paying male visitors and her lady-of-the-night glamour, was left unsupported. Over the years, Roisin wondered what violent tearing of the heart, torture of the mind, or temptation of the flesh ensued, impelling their mother to extricate herself from her children's lives forever … for eternity.

Their family unit tore apart, irretrievably broken, leaving their future uncertain. With no parental haven, the distraught and terrified Anna fled, leaving her babies behind. Her face bloodied, sliced by the knife in the hand of her enraged husband. The scar was quick to heal, but the festering wounds from never again seeing her children would last a lifetime. She went on to have three more children. Six babes in as many years.

Later in life, Roisin discovered that her mother was a bigamist, and her secrets were laid bare for all her children to see. Her father Seamus, on occasion, returned to his homeland and also spent time at Her Majesty's pleasure. The truth and the whys and wherefores of what led up to the separation of her warring parents, Roisin and her brother and sister being taken to live in Northern Ireland for a time, and then later separated by the English care system, would not be brought to light until many years after she was reunited with her father. What little information she received was drip-fed, mostly accidentally, or turned out to be a lie, told to satisfy her endless curiosity.

Roisin and her siblings' lives too would be blighted by their father's anger and violence, after they came to live with him in Highfields. He was unapproachable, driving young imaginations to invent their own versions of the truth. Years would pass before Roisin and her siblings would say their mother's name. Anna – four small letters that together created a simple word; but the thought or sound of that simple word became a gateway to a tumbling stream of whys, wheres and whens. The catalyst, the ignition of dejection that descended over Roisin, and corroboration of her mother's earthly existence arose from a delivery addressed to Roisin when she was twelve years old. She had never received a letter in the post before.

Darra, now lanky-legged, with ruffled hair and a toothless grin, stood close, wide-eyed in anticipation. Little Orla, her big brown cow eyes unblinking and fixated on the small white parcel, her clenched fists pressed over her mouth and nose. A postmark bearing the word Belfast and the date 1976 jumped out. Roisin turned over this cryptic gift, sensing an unknown consequence, staring down without expression, arms folded. Overseeing the event was their father. Biting her lip, Roisin gently prised open the corners of the sealed triangle. She fiddled for some time. A single item was retrieved, a crinkled black-and-white photo.

The huddled children leaned in, necks angling for a better view of the woman sitting cross-legged at the round bar table. She is wearing a plain, sleeveless, white summer dress; her body leaning slightly forward; her hands tugging at the edge of the hem, as if ensuring her modesty, or maybe attempting to hide a pregnancy. Roisin homed in on the woman's eyes: black, deeply intense, yet soulful and kind. Her eyebrows equally as black and pronounced, a considerable contrast to the mass of white hair tentatively bunched into a beehive and sitting proudly on top of her head. The ensemble completed with a simple black headband separating the bouffant from the neat straight fringe. Her long nails appear beautifully painted. There is no smile. There she sits, with an aura of abandoned vulnerability. At her side, cigarette tilted between his darkened, nicotine-stained fingers, sits their much younger father, his wedding ring patently visible. Ruggedly handsome, hair fashioned in the slicked-back, Teddy-boy look, he emanates confidence and control. Roisin hesitantly turned over the photo and voiced the written words, 'Anna, your mother!' Roisin knew it must have been Aunt Maeve who had sent this photo, but she did not know why. Maybe she felt guilty, or maybe her father was the one who was guilt-ridden, Roisin's constant questioning having finally got to him. She was happy to see the face of her mother; she knew she was out there somewhere and now she had the proof in her hand to keep forever.

After no time at all, Roisin, Darra and Orla, heads together, whispering under the bedcovers, agreed that their mother was either Myra Hindley, the monster who murdered little children, or their father had killed her and she was buried under the patio. Roisin kept the special photo hidden in the pages of her favourite book, *The Lion, the Witch and the Wardrobe*, and over the next few years, when she was feeling sad and lonely, needed to cry for help, or was trying to comfort Darra and Orla, she would take out that photo, look into her mother's eyes and plead, 'Where are you? Come and find us. Rescue us and take us away from Eileen, our jailer, Dad and this horrible house.'

There were many times when there was nowhere to run and hide and no one to turn to. Roisin and Orla shared a bedroom in their father's house. They would make a tent with a blanket stretched between the edge of the bed and the chest of drawers, and hide underneath, huddled together until they both stopped crying, or usually until Orla fell asleep. Darra had the smallest bedroom, so small his clothes were kept in a suitcase under his bed. Roisin, at twelve years old, had a good sense of what was right and wrong, and what was good and bad. She now knows what love and kindness feels like, and the three of them felt none of it in Highfields.

'Oh, how I miss Grandma Muggleton,' Roisin would say to Darra and Orla, remembering the sweet-natured, loving Mrs Muggleton, who was warm and cuddly and smelled of freshly baked cookies and garden flowers. 'Let's run away and find her. She must be searching for us. We need to leave … before they kill us, like our mother.' Darra and Orla were too young to understand, and too young to run away. Roisin knew it was impossible to leave, but she also knew the screaming, the beatings and punishments were wrong, and children should not be treated like dirty dogs and made to sit on the floor and made to stay silent and in fear of their lives. Over the next few years, thoughts of their mother coming to the rescue disappeared and the image of her became a bitter pill. The word 'mother' became meaningless. She became a non-entity.

With each punishment and episode of verbal abuse, Roisin changed. She began to feel smaller, crushed, and her forced silence was crippling. She lost her joy of reading and drawing and became withdrawn. Darra and Roisin began to argue and physically fight with each other, sometimes ending up with black eyes and bruises. They were traumatised and unable to cope with the oppression of their home life. Orla managed to escape most of the violence due to her big brown cow eyes and her lack of noise. She played endlessly with her dolls, brushing their hair and creating her own happy family moments.

One day, at school, Roisin met her new PE teacher, and her heart skipped a beat. The teacher's name was Anna Ball. She was from Huddersfield, she had a strong Yorkshire accent, long dark auburn hair, and big deep brown eyes. Roisin could not get past believing she could be her mother. She always had her favourite teachers and found herself trying to get close to them. She still needed saving. Every night before she went to sleep, Roisin would tuck Darra into bed, they would hug and say sorry to each other for any nasty words that had passed between them that day. Despite any anger, Roisin knew she wanted to save Darra. She and Orla would whisper their thoughts to one another in the safety of their bedroom, sharing secrets and often tears.

Many years later their father gave Darra a scrap of paper and on it was a printed address.

'Your grandad, Arthur Tweedy – your mother's father,' he said to Darra, shoving the note under his nose. 'He used to be a policeman, six foot four he was, married a woman called Glynis.' Roisin and Darra took the train, hoping they might find their mother, but fearing it was going to be a waste of time.

They arrived at number 10, a stone house in the middle of a row of stone houses that all looked the same, with small windows, a chimney, and a small grassy area at the front of the steep steps up to the front door. They stood fidgeting nervously behind the low stone wall at the front of the house, neither able to find the courage to open the black metal gate and walk up to the house. Suddenly, the net curtains begin to twitch and a moment later a petite grey-haired lady opened the front door. Glynis was flabbergasted and very much perturbed to find her late husband's grandchildren standing at her front door asking after him.

'You had best come in … but not for long. It's not right, just turning up like this,' she said in a troubled manner, leading them into a small kitchen with a wood-burning cooker.

Roisin and Darra followed behind, giving each other a blank look while simultaneously shrugging their shoulders. They had great difficulty understanding her Yorkshire dialect. 'Your grandad's gone. It fair broke his heart when your mother disappeared like that, just took off without telling a soul,' Glynis said, while trying to make hot chocolate drinks in a pan on the hob.

'We were just wondering,' Roisin uttered timidly, 'do you know where our mother is … and why she left us? And do you have any photos we can look at?' Darra sat uneasily, wringing his hands, desperate to drink the hot chocolate and skedaddle. Glynis left the kitchen and returned a few minutes later with a photo in her hand.

'That's my Arthur with you, Roisin. He was a grand chap … You must have been nowt but a few months old,' she said, managing a smile. Glynis handed them a hot chocolate each and then the tone in her voice turned abrasive. 'Nothing good will come from finding your mother. She's a bad 'un. We got a letter from your dad; he was trying to find her. The envelope had HMP stamped on it, so we knew where he was ... locked up. Now, time you went,' she said, slapping the photo into Roisin's hand. 'And if you find her, tell her there's nothing here for her. This is my house.'

The front door slammed shut, leaving Roisin and Darra stunned and feeling rejected.

Roisin was unsure whether she felt sorry for her mother, or just angry that the visit had been a waste of time. She had secretly hoped that Glynis was close to her, and she would come away with an address. She made her way back to Leicester with a heavy heart.

...

It was a sunny afternoon in June 2004. Roisin was wearing her favourite red halter-neck bikini and was drifting in and out of sleep while sunbathing in her garden when Orla called. Something in her voice made her sit up. Orla told her she knew where their mother was, she was living in Nottingham. Roisin threw her legs over the sun lounger and bent herself forwards, she needed a moment to compute the words she had just heard.

Orla told her she had written to the Salvation Army, and that they had managed to find her. She said she had already received a letter from their mother explaining that she wanted to meet her. With her head in her hands, Roisin tried to think about what to say next. She felt numb, a deathly silence fell over her thoughts and her emotions, there was no bubbling excitement or nagging curiosity – she told Orla she needed time to process what she wanted to do, if anything, with this new information.

...

A week later, Orla and her husband, Danny, visited Anna, their mother, and her daughter Tammy for afternoon tea. Roisin was at home, feeling restless, knowing her sister would soon be in the same room as their mother for the very first time. She tried to play out in her mind the moment they came face to face with one another, what they were each thinking and the first words that were spoken between them. Roisin had refused to visit her mother with Orla. The thought of it both horrified and nauseated her, but gnawing curiosity was now driving deep into her psyche ensuring their meeting consumed her thoughts. Orla wasn't one for conveying the drama of an event. She was overly nonchalant, and Roisin knew she would give her only the basics, putting her emotions aside. Roisin's thirst for the nitty gritty of how their mother looked and acted went unquenched. What followed was a week of internal deliberation. That the natural desire to be with her mother, which had haunted her throughout her whole life, could now be realised, if only she could reach out. What should she do?

Over the following weeks, Orla revealed more of how she felt, seeing, talking to and embracing her mother. 'I look just like her,' she said, her big brown eyes opening wider, 'just as Dad told me. She's very tall, and she's got long dark auburn hair, nothing like the peroxide blonde in our photo. She used to be a nurse … We met Tammy. She's nice.' The 'used to be a nurse' part struck a chord with Roisin. Having worked alongside many nurses as a physiotherapist, she thought them generally kind and giving people.

'So,' she ruminated, 'she must be a smart woman, kind and personable.'

Her interest in meeting her mother grew, and when Orla mentioned their mother and Tammy wanted to meet Orla's two girls, Annie and Jemma, and would be visiting her at the weekend, Roisin decided to be there. She waited with Orla, Danny and their two daughters, for the resounding crack of the brass doorknob hammering on the front door, a noise that would alert Roisin to the arrival of the person who had lived as a figment of her imagination as a child. A ghostly figure who she had called upon when soaked in tears, and bereft of tenderness, love and protection.

Roisin tried to keep her perspective, lessen her expectations of what kind of woman might walk through the door, the way she would look, her voice, her smell … It all felt so overwhelming. Her emotions flip-flopped from a deep need to let go, cry and embrace the woman whose heartbeat she needed to feel, to thinking about all the negative words and violent acts that were embedded into her memory from living with her father. Roisin was very much aware that for her, forgiveness and understanding of her mother's absence in their lives would not come easily.

The sound of two clanks from the front door brought Roisin and Orla to their feet. Roisin took a deep breath to release the tension in her mind and jaw. She was good at that, having had many experiences in life where she had to quickly mask her vulnerabilities and portray self-confidence and boldness. And there she was – her mother slowly walking toward her. Their eyes locked, transmitting between them a lifetime of intertwined thoughts and fears. They embraced each other for some time, Roisin resisting the urge to sob. Anna let her tears flow. It was a sobering moment for everyone in the room.

The angst and harsh thoughts drained away from Roisin in that instant. What surfaced initially was an open mind and heart, and a necessity to discover who this woman, her mother, was. Over the following year and four reunions, Roisin absorbed the puzzle and personality of her mother. It was a time of dredging, picking apart the pieces, seeing what fits and what does not sit well. It took time and a lot of self-reflection and analysis. It was a difficult journey; one Roisin became reluctant to continue. It was seeing photos on her mother's sideboard of two of her other children in their caps and gowns, flanked by their mother and father, looking loved and supported, holding their degree certificates on their graduation days that finally made her withdraw from forming a relationship with her mother. These images scorched the very core of her. Roisin concluded that if she could not be all in with open arms, the price was too high and her pain and resentment too entrenched, she had nothing more to give her mother.

Roisin found it difficult to get close to her mother. She saw the sadness in her eyes; they never lit up. She, too, was proficient at masking her vulnerabilities and keeping her secrets well hidden. Roisin and Orla felt cheated of the truth. Their mother did heap the blame on their father, and she had a right to do so, given where she had stood as a nineteen-year-old. But Roisin thought she should have searched for them and done everything in her power to ensure her children were safe and away from the man she, too, had to hide from.

The last time Roisin saw her mother, she told her that she had fostered many children. Maybe she thought that by mentioning this, Roisin would see her as compassionate – it had the opposite effect. Roisin only felt anger towards her mother, knowing she had invested her time and her affections on other children, after leaving her own to fend for themselves. Roisin walked away – not because she wanted to punish her mother, but because she needed to stop the hurt she was feeling and to put the past to bed. Roisin still felt like her twelve-year-old self, holding the black-and-white photo of her mother in her hand, hoping that one day an angel would appear and she would be made whole. Long before she met James, Roisin realised that all the love and guidance her mother gave to her fostered children only helped her forget the ones she had birthed.

It was many years later, during the Christmas season of 2022, that Orla told Roisin and Darra that their mother had cancer and may not have long to live. Feeling conflicted about the rights and wrongs of the decisions she had made such a long time ago regarding her mother, Roisin descended back into the past, trying to justify her reasons for turning her back on her mother. This time, choosing never to see her mother again must be a decision she could live with for the rest of her life. She had seen her mother's tears, she was real, not imagined and this might be her final show. Darra did not feel the impulse to see his mother before she died, but he did not escape the deafening cries demanding he come to terms with his past. Shortly after hearing of her diagnosis, he had a breakdown. Orla wanted to say goodbye to her mother and attended her funeral.

Roisin just wanted to move on and forget – it was easier for her to let go of a 'cold' memory, than make a new one, a long lasting, sad and tearful farewell.

At fifty-seven, Roisin had finally come to terms with the mother in her head, the mother in her reality, and the mother she never became – but being a mother to Noah remained a wound that she knew would haunt her until her last breath.

Our Right

The corridor we rove boasts only momentary thought
Yearning, reaching, inferring a vision never to find
Breaking free from regulation, the adult way we're
    taught
Asphyxiated, agonised, within adolescent mind
Ineptly, lumberingly, unseeingly, rendering our own
    direction
Freedom from blame, our innocence, a friability raw
Lost and alone, begging doting parental protection
Our susceptibility, our childness, we entreat do
    not ignore
Give attention to our whimpers, our importune
    for love
Just as night's shadow fades with bathing morning
    light
Shield, tend father and mother, oh ... the lack
    thereof
You conceived, you nurtured, inculcate the need
    to fight
Your life, your will, your incumbrance to endure
Our right for guidance, our right for truth
Our right not to pass by the child ... our youth.

                              Roisin, August 2005

10

NO BRAKE ON A WRECKING BALL

Roisin remembers writing the poem 'Our Right' in 2005, after she had concluded that she did not want to see her mother again before she passed away. It was because she felt so indifferent to her. Her mother was a stranger and there was no meeting of minds, no sense that there was anything there to salvage. It was too painful going back to her past and her absent mother was her past. Orla needed something Roisin didn't need: a grandmother for her children, and she wanted her mother to become her friend. Roisin watched Orla put a lot of time into forging a friendship with their mother, but it never came to be. Orla, too, came away from her presence conflicted, feeling let down and left to recall her own childhood sadness.

Knowing Orla's vulnerabilities, Roisin does not feel it is right to lean on her sister now her marriage is in distress. Orla has had very little experience in negotiating relationships, and Roisin thinks she would tell her to leave James. And maybe she's not ready to hear the truth. She thinks back previously, to a day in 1974, when her brother and sister were following behind her. They had left Mrs Muggleton's house and arrived at the flat where their father and his girlfriend Eileen were living.

Roisin got to the top of the concrete steps, leaving the stench of urine in the stairway and corridors behind her. Darra and Orla were much slower to reach the second floor of the housing block. She dumped her heavy school bag on the stone floor by the railing and waited for them to turn the last corner. Their faces were red with exhaustion and screwed up because of the awful smells. She looked down towards the two people standing in front of the last one of six doors. She beckoned her siblings to walk behind her to the end of the long balcony, which had a black metal railing on one side, a barrier stopping them from falling over the edge.

A man with a big bushy gingery beard and wearing a white tee shirt and jeans, stood smiling, opened armed and ready to greet them.

'I'm ya da … Come you three in,' he said in a Northern Irish accent, 'and this is your stepma, Eileen.' Roisin just followed orders and walked into the small flat, towards the big windows that looked over St Peter's estate. Her face showed them how much she felt detached from her surroundings, her father and the woman standing next to him. Darra walked through a lot more enthusiastically, dropped his bag on the brown carpet, climbed on the settee and started to jump up and down giggling. Until he was suddenly and forcibly thrown off his feet and pushed face down into the seat cushions by his father's hand grasping the scruff of the back of his jumper. 'Ya don't do that here, laddie,' he said in a deep voice, and with a forbidding look.

Clutching onto her pink schoolbag in front of her with both hands, Orla took a tentative step backwards. Eileen stood with pursed lips, each hand curled into a fist and resting on her hips. She shot a cold gawp at Roisin, who held her stare.

'Up the stairs then. I'll show you your bedrooms,' she said, matter of fact, as if instructing them to a cell. Roisin heard a jangle of keys and saw them swinging from side to side from a loop on Eileen's trousers as she walked in front of her up the stairs. When Roisin noticed all three bedroom doors had a small padlock on them, her heart sank. Their bedroom was a cell. Over the two weeks that followed, the children had to learn the rules that they had to obey. 'Bedrooms are locked until bedtime, unless you are inside. Under punishment, no food upstairs. Children are dirty therefore you sit on the floor when downstairs. Do not open the windows.' They, too, had locks on them.

'Roisin and Darra, you must wash all the school clothes and bed linen in the bath with your feet and hang them on the line. No noise when the telly is on. And you must never go into your father's and my bedroom. If I catch you by the door being nosy, you will be locked in the cupboard under the stairs for days.' Eileen always dished out the rules, and she added new ones each day, whatever suited her mood. She carried out her role as jailer with relish, and she never relaxed or overlooked a 'transgression'.

Roisin thought Eileen reasonably attractive when she first met her. Initially, her long, sandy-coloured hair looked soft and flowy, and her big, bluey-grey eyes flickered an occasional twinkle. But as the weeks went by, her eyes darkened, becoming hollow, showing only intolerance and the potential for cruelty and her hair became scraggly and wild as the witchiest witch. Roisin watched as their father, who she had not yet come to know, remained quiet, never questioning the rules or the drill commands of the jailer. His willingness to sanction punishments, both verbal and physical, unflinchingly and without sorrow or remorse, was something the children would never be able to come to terms with.

'Seamus, Seamus!' she would scream, with both her hands over her forehead, her fingers clawing at her flesh, leaving trails of blood. 'The little bastards, they're getting on my nerves. Make them shut up,' she would screech like a wailing cat, rocking her head back and forth. Their father would charge in like an angry bear rounding up his foe, thrashing his fists about their heads and plunging them into their den with a hot breathy growl and a slamming shut of the exit route. His fists would plunge with fury into whatever bodily part came into their path. The back of the head was his preferred target where hair could hide the bruises. He was like a wrecking ball swinging into action, smashing whatever stood in his way until crushed and on its knees.

Eileen would oversee the beatings with a folding of her arms and a minacious gloat. She always wore dark Crimplene trousers and a loose-fitting short-sleeved top that revealed her unsupported sagging breasts as they shifted from side to side just above the waistband of her slacks. She liked everyone to see the self-inflicted slash wounds on her forearms. She told everyone who would listen of her diagnosed schizophrenia, insufferable pain and her stoicism in taking on three feral children. Mostly, Roisin thought, so that everyone would walk on eggshells around her and not dare to challenge her in even the simplest way. Behind closed doors, she was a monster. The children didn't dare let a single vulgar word leave their mouths, or a single defiant look cross their faces. They knew better; the consequences were too great.

Their fear became palpable, waiting for a whack on the back of the head from a frying pan, a forceful yank of the hair, a barrage of abuse after a minor slip up or a night spent locked in the cupboard under the stairs. Eileen did not have a job. Instead, she was always at home calculating, ensuring the children were locked out of the flat in all weathers, fending for themselves all weekend, and seven days a week on school holidays. And still she managed to have a naughty list to rant about every evening, when their father walked through the front door after work. His return home usually started with a sharp smack on the back of the head of each child as they tentatively entered the flat and ran the gauntlet, twisting and turning, hoping to outwit his blows.

Roisin will never forget waiting to see their father enter the concrete housing block, so she and her siblings could run up the stairs, huddle together nursing their hunger, each evening in the smelly stairway, negotiating who would be the first to open the front door. If they did not return in time for when dinner was served to their father, there was not a second chance, and the first smack was always the hardest. Roisin remembers how they endured four years of physical and emotional harm, inflicted at the hands and mouths of their father and Eileen. Eileen's frequent screaming outbursts and displays of self-harm led Roisin, from the age of twelve, to stay at Laurette's flat next door at weekends and on some school nights, babysitting her two children, Kory and Kiana.

Laurette always asked about the last row she had heard, the crying and the shouting. She knew what was happening and she made her home available as a place of refuge. She gave Roisin pocket money, and she also gave her a voice of reason. Her flat was decorated with African art, with animal-print wallpaper and elephant designs on the cushions and throws. There was a Zulu shield and spear above the dark chocolate velvet settee and a zebra-skin rug on the floor, which Roisin tried to avoid stepping on. Laurette's bedroom looked even more wild. The bedside lamp was deep red, its hue washed over a brown blanket spread over the large bed. In the centre lay a dramatic image of a tiger's head with its mouth wide open, baring a full set of sharp teeth.

While Roisin entertained Laurette's children, Laurette entertained any number of men in her jungle room, as Roisin liked to call it. Roisin would snigger to herself when hearing the noises the animals made, the howling wolfs, the grunting gorillas, the laughing hyenas. She liked Laurette a lot and thought very little of the nature of these visits. It was a secret they shared, and it felt special. When a man knocked on the front door, she would look at him through the kitchen window and think to herself, 'I bet he will be a donkey,' or an elephant or maybe a monkey.

Roisin knew nothing of sex at this age, but she did think whatever Laurette was doing in her bedroom sounded a lot of fun and the men always left smiling, giving Laurette many cuddles and kisses goodbye. This was love, she thought. When Bembe, Laurette's younger brother, came home from work and knew his sister was having fun in her bedroom, he would call Roisin up to the bathroom. It was a routine she was familiar with. She watched him undress. She thought he had the loveliest smile she had ever seen, big brown teddy-bear eyes and soft fuzzy hair that she loved to twizzle in her fingers. She looked up at him. He was so tall, so handsome and he pulled funny faces and made giggly noises, putting his finger to his mouth as he looked down at her, as if reminding her that this was their big secret, their special time.

He would jump in the bath, his body then mostly covered with frothy bubbles. He looked so happy with his eyes closed, smiling with his hand wrapped round what Roisin thought looked like a big brown sausage. He moved his hand slowly up and down, and she put both her hands around the top of the sausage just like he showed her, and she gently squeezed, and they both went up and down together until he groaned like the men in Laurette's bedroom.

'Thank you, my lovely secret girlfriend,' Bembe would say, reaching over the bath, puckering up his lips for Roisin to kiss him. She always left the bathroom feeling happy. He was her special friend.

Years later, Orla told her that she, too, had become Bembe's special friend when she turned twelve. The strange thing was that neither of them saw it as child abuse. They compared notes and Orla decided that as she had been given a ten pence piece afterwards, she had done a better job. They shared an uneasy laugh together and then Orla said she would have killed anyone who touched her daughters. They looked at each other in horror at the thought. Roisin now recognises that what happened to her and her sister was child abuse and responsible for the distorted views on sex and love that she developed during her childhood and young adult life. Child abuse had damaged her in so many ways.

She also recognises now that her father and Eileen were responsible for destroying any hope of having a family of her own. What she learnt from their abuse was that adults and children cannot live together, and that emotional pain lasts longer than physical pain, and that there is no fairy tale together, only survival alone. She recalls feeling desensitised to the frequent verbal and physical abuse from their father and Eileen. Roisin and Darra took the beatings and stood fast before their aggressors, their tears dry, their defiance beginning to show. For Darra, it was a clenching of his fists, an angry stare, a slow walk out of the flat. Roisin, at thirteen years of age, started to try to negotiate with her father and Eileen, telling them that there was a better way and that beating and swearing at a child was wrong.

She became more despondent as their relationships broke down further and the violence stepped up and became more destructive. The mind games and vitriolic language pushed Roisin into an even darker place. The days were awash with angst, shame and blame. Roisin saw her father as incomprehensible and she feared him.

Roisin remembers clearly one evening when Eileen went into one of her rages. She caught Darra outside her bedroom door, touching a padlock she had fitted. She grabbed their father's belt from his jeans, which he always left hanging over the stair rail, and began beating him on his naked legs, continuing even when he screamed and begged for her to stop. Roisin ran from the living room to the bottom of the stairs and saw the viciousness in Eileen's screwed-up face and steely eyes. She was holding his wrist tight while he wriggled and squirmed, trying to get away from the lashing that rained down upon his bare skin, now red raw where the leather had whipped into his flesh. Roisin, sobbing, pleaded with their father to stop Eileen. Roisin can still see her father now, sitting on his chair. He never flinched nor lowered the newspaper he was reading.

Later that night, Roisin soaked a flannel in cold water and tried to ease the smarting on Darra's legs.

'I'm going to run away,' Darra kept saying again and again in between his crying. After some time, she tiptoed to her bedroom and lay her drowsy head on the pillow, trying to fall asleep to the sound of Darra weeping and the voices in her mind going over their plan to run away together the next day. Dressed in their school uniforms, they spent the day walking, with no idea of where they were going, for what they thought seemed like a very long way. It was a dry, sunny day, and they spent hours sitting around and saying very little to each other. They found themselves in the village of Oadby and, as day turned to night, they huddled together in the stairwell of an apartment building.

Roisin remembers that night as if it were yesterday. They stayed awake all night, feeling sick and shivering from the cold. Darra moaned all night long that he wanted to go back. At first light, they left the building and walked past a man who was piling bundles of newspapers from a van into the post office doorway.

'Eh up, what are you two doing here at five in the morning?' he shouted, with a puzzled look on his face. Roisin and Darra quickly ran across the road to distance themselves from the stranger, trying to retrace their tracks from the day before. After a few minutes, a police car pulled alongside them and stopped. Darra was shaking with the cold, and looked pale and sickly. He turned to Roisin, his eyes full of sadness, looking for permission to talk to the policeman.

'Let's go home, Darra,' she said, feeling defeated and helpless.

Back at home, after an aggressive rant about embarrassment and being put to bed with a bash on the back of the head, Darra, too, became silent. He distanced himself from Roisin. He shrank away, always sitting in the corner of his bedroom on the floor with his head between his knees, rocking. He stopped bothering to keep himself clean and tidy, and he bunked off school. He no longer agreed to wash the sheets in the bath, so Roisin vowed to do his share while he was unwell. She would often push open his bedroom door slowly, peeping in to check on him. Mostly, he was wrapped up in an old, thin, light blue, bobbled blanket, like a bug in a cocoon, his spotty greasy face and unwashed hair poking out the top.

During this period, Orla found some comfort with their father. He noticed how cute she was, her beautiful big brown eyes and straight-cut fringe framing her impish face. She gave him no trouble and she began to win him over with her soft way and her outreached arms. He even made up a little rhyme and would let her sit on his knee.

'Oh, my little Orla, my wee Irish girl. Show ya da now, how you do a little twirl.'

Roisin was pleased Orla had tempered the ogre and found the attention she so needed, but she could not calm his violent nature. Having tried and failed to show him love, her older, wiser head warned her that placating him was futile and he would still break her. Roisin's attitude to her father never changed and he remained wary of her until his last breath, jealous even of her strength and fortitude. She remembers squaring up to him when she was in her twenties after he lunged at her with a raised hand, suggesting the red lipstick she was wearing made her look like a prostitute. She clenched her fists and faced him off, snarling at him, letting him know, 'this fucking bitch fights back now … she's no longer a child'.

Eileen began to spend days in her bedroom, emerging with new deep scratches and wounds on her face and arms. She wailed and told the children of her suffering, how they had ruined her life.

'You little whore, you jealous little bitch … If it wasn't for you,' she would shout, spitting out her words with her saliva spraying on Roisin's face, laughing like a mad woman one minute, then sobbing the next. Roisin had no understanding of her illness; she just thought of her as mad and filled with hatred. 'I don't want you kids in my house,' she would bellow, furiously wagging her witchy finger. 'You're here because of your dad. You make me sick the way you stare at me, acting all self-righteous and … so important.

You're nothing and you'll always be nothing.' Roisin offered no response to her vile words, she just stood still, staring hard at her, waiting for her to run out of steam and saunter off, hoping she would cut deeper into her wrists this time, and bleed out and die.

Even now Roisin cannot forgive or forget the event that began one day when Eileen was in the kitchen, prodding Roisin on her chest in the kitchen, telling her how useless she was. Her vexed eyes bulged behind her thick black-rimmed glasses as she spat her anger out into Roisin's face, even more vehemently these days as she did not get the crumpled, distraught response she was looking for. As she smacked Roisin around the face and then held a handful of her hair as she swung her from side to side, Darra finally cracked. Taking a knife out of the kitchen drawer, he held it against Eileen's throat. In a rage, he spat at her, 'Stop, you ugly cow,' he snarled. 'Let her go, you evil witch.'

Eileen lifted her arm in defence, trying to dislodge the knife that was now pushing against her skin. Roisin grasped the moment and threw a strong punch into the side of Eileen's head. Eileen went down and lay bent over on the floor, covering her head with both her hands. Darra and Roisin began kicking her body. On hearing the screams, their father charged in and, without hesitation, grasped hold of Roisin's hair with one hand and the neck of her jumper with the other. He then dragged her, kicking and screaming, along the kitchen floor into the living room, where he yanked her onto the chair. Her eyes were red, pleading for him to let her go, but his hands squeezed harder and harder around her neck, pushing her head over the arm of the chair. Her voice would no longer beg, her breath began to escape her. The image of her father's clenched teeth and red face, Darra trying to pull him off and Orla standing next to him crying faded away.

Her hands, no longer pleading for her father's release, lay flaccid, her head hung backwards. Darra watched their father slam the front door behind him and lifted Roisin's head onto the back support of the chair. His reddened, tearful face was the first she saw. He helped her stand and climb the stairs. After the savage strangulation, Roisin, aged fourteen, knew she had to run from the extremes of her aberrant family life. Still fraught from abuse, she packed a bag. Eileen stood in the hallway with her arms folded, watching Roisin and Darra as they walked down the stairs.

'You'll never win. Your dad will always put me first,' she said, cackling with cynicism, as if she found the drama satisfying. Darra left the flat and went to a friend's house.

Roisin remembers suffering four fractured years, clawing at scraps of pitiful paternal affection. The damage was done, she had no expectation of happiness. She was broken, and survival was her overriding thought. With her gone, she hoped that her brother and sister might have a chance to receive the prize of favouritism and a moment's love. Darra and Roisin promised to keep in touch. Throughout the violent event, no one gave comfort to Orla, the young girl left distraught and sobbing in the corner of the living room. Roisin did not see her siblings again for a few weeks. Roisin, still very much a tomboy, with thick, messy, short red hair flopping over her face and ears, and her nails chewed down to the quick and bleeding, wearing scruffy jeans and a ripped tee shirt, her neck still red and bruised, her face stained with tears, sprinted to her friend's house.

Ciara Slaney, Roisin's friend from school, lived alone with her father. He seemed only able to exist in his reclining chair and in a bottle of whiskey. Ciara told Roisin she could live with her; her dad never questioned the arrangement. Roisin smiles to herself as she recalls this time in her life, her rebel-yell moment. Roisin and Ciara dyed each other's hair black and then spiked it, and spent every day loitering around Leicester's Haymarket Shopping Centre, once stealing two pairs of monkey boots. In the evening, they would make up their faces with black zig-zag patterns and red lipstick and go crazy listening and pogoing to the punk rock sounds of the Sex Pistols and The Damned in Ciara's bedroom. Cigarette in hand, singing the words to Billy Idol's hit song, 'Rebel Yell'. Jumping from the bed to the chair, dancing with a big old teddy bear and a pretend microphone, sharing a bottle of Ciara's old man's cider. For a time, Roisin felt free.

This rebellious purging only lasted six weeks. Instilled in her by her compassionate foster parent, Mrs Muggleton, was the need to receive and show kindness, to learn and to teach, to reach out for peace. After accepting a gift, a Bible from a friend she had become close to at school, she decided to study with her friend in the park once a week. Roisin straightened herself out, stopped bunking off school and encouraged Ciara to follow her lead.

Roisin only finds one photo relating to this time, a photo of herself looking like a snotty tomboy, but she does find a poem that she remembers writing before her father strangled her.

Angry Bear No More

Father, you are so big, you are so scary
Your eyes like ice-blue sapphires, so cold and staring
Your coarse ginger beard and unruly head of hair
The waves of hair coating your body, the grunts
    and groans
Your smile that we never trust, for fear you are a
    hungry bear
Too afraid to approach you, as our den we solemnly
    roam
What we want is Winnie the Pooh, soft and
    sweet-natured as honey
A big cuddle who likes to play in the woods and
    romp in the grass
Big protective paws that scoop us up, keeping us safe
    from the witch
Please, angry bear, no more, no hurting fist, no more
    crying bairn to grasp
And so, we may burrow into your heart, finding
    your goodness and there enrich

                              Roisin, 1978

11

WEREWOLF

Roisin cannot recall a day when she, Darra or Orla were taken by their father to a beach, around a fair or to any other children's entertainment places. She wonders if perhaps he did, and she has blocked it out because of a reluctance to let go of her hurt and pain. Maybe she is unable to see her father as anything but distant and mean. Or, is it simply that her memories have faded and blurred over time?

She does, though, remember distinctly and vividly the one moment when she sat close to her father on the settee, not holding on to him or touching his skin, just her legs touching his legs. At the time, he was wearing shorts. That simple act of closeness sparked something in her mind which, later in the deepness of sleep became a nightmare that frequently found its way into her slumber and her daydreams over the years.

The thirteen-year-old Roisin could hear no sound in her dream, there was no movement of limbs.

She was focused on her father's hand resting on his thigh, the one closest to her leg. His fingers were like big fat sausages, but very hairy, and with nails that were bitten to the quick. The sides of his first two fingers, where he held a cigarette, were brown with nicotine stains. She stared at his hand, the same hand that had slapped her across the face the day before and left a red mark on her cheek, the hand that always grabbed her by her red hair, pulling her back and onto the floor, stopping her from getting away from him. Suddenly, the hair on his hand began to move, slowly at first, then growing quickly, becoming darker and thicker, gathering speed, and spreading over his fat fingers, covering the brown stains until they could no longer be seen.

His whole hand became a huge black paw with large sharp claws growing out from the top of each finger. The thick black hair, now like a tsunami, rushed over his thigh, completely covering his leg. In that instant, all at once and in a grip of panic, she turned and faced her father … The hot searing breath and dripping blood of a werewolf's fangs and open mouth engulfed her face, viciously tearing at her flesh. She suddenly opened her eyes wide in sheer terror at the sight of her father pressing a hot damp flannel on her forehead. He told her in an unfamiliar, softer voice that she was having another bad dream. He tied his trouser belt around her head to keep the flannel in place and left her bedroom. Roisin tried to calm herself, longing for her banging headache to pass. She remembers this sole act of paternal care; it was usually not the way with him.

Her father was neither a boozer, nor a womaniser; he was just an angry man who thought he deserved more and had allowed bitterness to rot his faith and the good he had in his life. He worked long hours in a factory and had always longed for the finer things in life and a bank balance that would give him whatever he wanted. Saturday nights, he would put on his gold rings, his best bib and tucker and a three-quarter-length black coat with its collar turned up. The image Roisin remembers of him most was him walking out the front door, head down low, with a lit cigarette resting precariously between his lips and a gangster's swagger.

Roisin has never known him to put another's needs before his own or to share anything, including his time. Most of his decisions relating to his own children were mistakes and most of his actions were damaging. He turned out to be a better grandfather – to Orla's first-born Annie. Once he knew he was dying, he wanted Roisin to deal with the health professionals regarding his treatment. She knew this was because she was less emotionally invested in him and her medical degree afforded her a pragmatic and forthright approach with consultants. Roisin clearly remembers the circumstances around the time his bowel cancer became known to him. He had just returned home from a holiday in Cyprus with his lady friend Bridie.

His tan accentuated his large, perfectly straight white teeth, his golden eyebrows, and his strikingly blue eyes. Orla commented on how he looked a picture of health and so much younger than his sixty-two years. There was no indication of his impending diagnosis and need for immediate lifesaving surgery. During the first night after he had arrived home, he began to feel an extreme, incapacitating pain in his abdomen to the point he collapsed. He was told he had bowel cancer. Roisin stood facing the scan highlighted on the whiteboard and saw the tumours throughout his liver. When she walked into his hospital room, her face told him he was out of options. Over the next fourteen months, he declined into a suffering, wizened old man. He never said much about anything, only the practicalities of his needs.

There was no 'if only this' or 'what if that'. She dared not bring up the subject of money, his house or his will. He was bitter enough. He saw his visiting children as vultures circling his bed. The three of them still needed to prove their worth. He pitted one against the other. They all knew they were only as good as the last thing they had done for him. Roisin was at university during his last few years. Her last few months of study entailed-finishing a dissertation, completing a caseload management project, having artificial insemination at a fertility clinic and looking after her father's dog Twiglet, all while her relationship with Andreas was breaking up and her father required easy-exit planning, which he refused daily, especially the last rights by a priest brought in by his insistent sister, Maeve. With his last throw at life, he shouted at the priest telling him to 'Fuck off until I'm dead and gone – and on my way.'

Roisin and her brother and sister were all there by his side when he died. They each told him they loved him and said goodbye. Roisin, Darra and Orla did not bond during this time, rather they dealt with his death each in their own way. It was years later that Roisin thought more about her father's life from his perspective. She felt he had never known real happiness, or true love in his life. He died young, never openly able to love, or be loved, to forgive or be forgiven. His children never did see their father cry, nor reflect. He thought being their father in name was enough.

Roisin never visited his grave but, after his death, his children became unburdened and closer to one another. The trauma of him never left Roisin and Darra. Even in their late fifties, they still find themselves regurgitating his behaviour and effect on them. Orla, not so much in the firing line, saw him mellow with age, and be a loving grandfather to her two children, and she allowed herself to forgive for the rest.

When Roisin, aged fifty-six, heard the words of James Blunt's song 'Monsters' for the first time after going to one of his concerts, a flood of emotion and memory consumed her. 'That's how I wanted to feel about you, Dad,' her heart screamed. The words of the song were so poignant and like an arrow shot to her heart – not for the beautiful love James Blunt expresses for his father, but for the beautiful love she never had, and had missed from a father. Her own father left a pain that could be elicited at the thought of him, speaking of him, or hearing a word of him … a wrenching of her guts, as if a hand had reached into the bowels of her, pulling her insides out … and all she can remember of him are fear and snarling teeth.

12

HUSH-A-BYE

Roisin thinks of Orla. She knows Saturdays are her favourite day and she will be spending the day at home. Roisin is so pleased that her sister achieved the job that she had always wanted in life. When Orla was a child, Roisin would watch her playing with her dolls for hours, brushing and styling their hair. She always thought she would become a hairdresser. Roisin also feels happy for her sister, knowing she has everything she needs at home: her husband Danny, who she loves very much, and two daughters Annie and Jemma, who mean the world to her.

Despite Orla's present contentment, Roisin is aware that her sister's abandonment issues are still raw. Over the years, Roisin has come to see that running away was never an option for Orla. She watched Orla take responsibility for their difficult father until he died, and she faced motherhood with no experience to call upon. Roisin was surprised when she bravely searched for and contacted the mother who had left her when she was still in nappies. Roisin thinks that, over the years, her sister has tried to fill the empty void in her broken heart by trying to fix what had happened to her in the past, whereas she wanted to get away from what was breaking her. Roisin remembers Orla, as a child, being so tiny, always afraid and hiding her cute China-doll face and big brown cow eyes under a blanket. She remembers her mostly just being there, silent and taking in everything that was happening around her.

It wasn't until Orla was in her fifties, and they had become much closer, that Orla finally opened up to Roisin and told her of some of the memories and feelings that she had kept buried for so long. At the age of ten, Orla had witnessed the streaming red blood drip from Eileen's wrist onto the white bathroom sink as she cut into her skin. She stood still in the doorway, watching her slash her wrist, and as the blood flowed faster, she did not call her dad, but went into her bedroom and played with her dolls as if nothing had happened. She remembered later feeling like there was something wrong with her and that she was not normal.

Roisin recalls Orla standing amid the screaming and the violence. No one paid any notice to her fear. Everyone, including Roisin, would tell Orla to hush, be quiet, go over there and cry. Shush, shush before I hit you, shush, shush before they hit you. There was never a sweet hush-a-bye baby, sleep well. Poor Orla never knew who to turn to for comfort. Her love and loyalty bounced around, seeking out safety. Roisin saw how Orla, as a young woman, stayed close to their father, only to feel his wrath and disapproval.

Orla had told Roisin of his harsh words and constant demands, and she told Orla to fight back and stop looking after him, but she felt crushed, and at that time did not have the maturity to find another way. She was lonely, childlike and lost, never knowing how to grow, or how to fit in. She found herself in a dark place, wanting closure. Social services were alerted by a schoolteacher, and they took a closer look. She went on to spend four weeks in hospital, unravelling what was tearing her apart. Roisin, far away, was busy making her own mistakes at this time, and never knew what her sister was going through.

Roisin was so happy to see that as the years went by, and Danny Miles came into her sister's life, her dry and sparky wit began to shine through. They got married and had two beautiful girls, and motherhood was the making of her. Orla wanted so much more, but the way forward seemed too challenging. She felt safer in a smaller world, protecting her soft and fragile heart and those she loved.

Roisin recalls the many times when Orla saved Roisin, supporting her at the fertility clinic and through the trauma of trying to keep her pregnancy a secret. And then the evening when she and Danny helped Roisin move all her worldly goods to her new house, when she left Andreas in the dead of the night. The two sisters' paths have criss-crossed over the years, and even though their adult lives are now so different, and they are opposite in many ways, the need to have each other in their lives has always been strong. With the passing of time, they have come to see their past behind them and their future ahead as one story.

13

THROW CAUTION TO THE WIND

The present, Saturday, 2 p.m.

Vivi and Arrabella turn up at Roisin's house uninvited. Not knowing the intercom code and wanting to surprise her, they decide to scramble over the front gate, giggling uncontrollably as they heave their butts clumsily over the top, to the sound of passing cars and their beeping horns,. Dodging the ferocious guard dogs while swinging a champagne bottle and a Neuhaus History Collection chocolate box, they sprint into the porch, Vivi shouting excitedly,

'We are going to London!'

Roisin opens her front door to see Arrabella staring back at her, attempting to pull down the hem of her skirt to her knees, and Vivi in her favoured sex-kitten, figure-hugging black leggings, which show off her chub-free youthful upper-inner thighs. On her pouty lips are the words, 'Here I am!' and on her face, as always, one of her 'I'm up to no good' devilish looks.

'It's Saturday and we are staying at my Mayfair house for a wild one,' she says, raising her eyebrows, and smirking as she saunters through to the kitchen, demanding the appropriate glasses to accompany the Tattinger.

'You know I was hoping for a quiet weekend. Did you not get the email?' Roisin questions, pleading. Arrabella, plus champagne and chocolates, charges straight upstairs through to Roisin's dressing room. Vivi follows, also with a glass of bubbles, some of it spilling over the rim and onto the pure wool, oyster stairs carpet, as she encourages Roisin with a few gentle nudges in the desired direction.

Arrabella, already rummaging through Roisin's glam evening collection, contorts a few 'maybe', and a few 'definitely not' faces.

Vivi interrupts, 'It has to be slutty enough for the Mayfair Club De Reve lap dancing club,' then pouts her lips, savouring a swallow of fizz.

'Fuck James, Roisin,' Arrabella says, shaking her head, placing her hand on Roisin's cheek, wiping away a tear. 'You need to stop looking at those photos on the bed. They will only make you miserable. This is the one,' she says, placing a cocktail dress against Roisin's body. 'Red and glitzy, to match your gorgeous fiery long hair and the Celtic goddess we know and love.'

Roisin was never going to out-talk Arrabella and Vivi, she concedes reluctantly after Vivi has her personal chauffer turn up at the house. Once sitting comfortably in the Mercedes-Benz S-Class, Roisin is feeling quite grateful and less maudlin about the state of her marriage and her dilemma. She welcomes the distraction of champagne, chocolates and her free and fanciful girlfriends rescuing her. And tonight, for once, she will not be thinking about James.

Vivi sashays past the queuing crowd like a goddess, with her head held high, her long glossy bistre hair whooshing from side to side and her peachy bottom winking at all those she is leaving behind. The burly doorman simply nods his head as he opens the door, allowing the group to pass without question.

Immediately Roisin's senses come to life at the sound and feeling of the boom, boom beat of the music resonating through her body. The last time she was in a nightclub was in her mid-twenties. Back then she was the belle of the ball, and she loved to dance and soak up the party scene.

'What you need, Roisin, is a double Hendrick's and a shot of XO brandy. It always loosens your legs on the ski slopes, and you look terrified,' Vivi shouts down her ear. Two hours later, after watching writhing, sexy bodies of babes wrapping themselves athletically and seductively around a stiff pole, downing drink after drink and thinking with her loins and not her head, Roisin finds her mojo, her courage not to care about tomorrow, to put aside her age and sensibilities and to look like she owns it.

As the night goes on, the club descends into a sweaty, steaming mass of gyrating bodies, seen through the changing colours, flashing lights and dry-ice clouds. Then Vivi makes her move, mouthing and beckoning to two late-twenty-somethings, well-groomed, square-jawed, perfect guns and pecs guys.

'Do bring your cute butts over here, boys.' They both swagger over like they are crushing a walnut between their bum cheeks. Packing fully charged egos, they claim to be hotshots in finance, and acquainted with the celebrity high-society jet-set crew. Vivi suggests to Roisin and Arrabella that she is very well versed in the art of posh-boy bunkum, and hopes their balls are more durable than their bank balances.

Clearly seeing the benefits of hooking up with three cougars, the young bucks, bubbly in hand, willingly surrender themselves to three drunk rich bitches, dragging them into a den of iniquity. Standing on a higher level, the latino-esque dancer gyrates suggestively, her red lipstick and red silk bodice well-defined, amid the mystery and blur of the seedy ambience, the black velvet walls, ceiling and poorly lit private booth. The hum and ride of the sensual music stokes up the mood to let it all go. The boys begin to grab handfuls of breasts, lifting dresses, their hands and fingers finding their way to pleasure the ladies. They begin to grind their hardened bulges into opening legs, pushing Vivi and Roisin against the wall. Arrabella steps back as she watches Vivi release the eager pythons and get to work.

Roisin also steps back for a moment, feeling this is who she used to be many years ago. She questions what she is doing here. Is it revenge for what James has done? She is carried away with the pleasure and wildness of Vivi rather than the men's bodies.

'Not here to fuck, boys, only play with you.' Vivi takes control of the show. Vivi gets to play with the meat. Roisin, encouraged by Vivi's delight, perches herself behind the toned hams and between two pairs of de-trousered, muscled-up, hairy thighs. Resting on her knees, facing Vivi, she finds herself well positioned to admire her friend's well honed, proficient and rather robust handling of two writhing parts.

Roisin firmly digs her nails into the two hardening buttocks and then juggles two pairs of jiggling balls charily with the patience and pose of a praying nun, contemplating the first, and the much later second, coming of Christ. Roisin notices Arrabella standing in the shadows and wonders what her friend thinks of her now. The three women, tumbling together, head to the exit, entwined in a drunken display of naked flailing arms and long-stockinged high-heeled legs, wearing little but a waggish look. They laugh riotously as they catch sight of the two probably-Eton boys, centre stage amid a testosterone scrum, no doubt bragging of their fortunate escapade. A tale the ladies know has long legs and will grow in sensationalism and sexual conquest with time.

In their morning negligees, popping paracetamols, the cougars swear a Pinky promise never to tell. Vivi goes back to bed and her chauffeur takes a very sleepy Arrabella and Roisin back to Barston village.

The present, Sunday, midday

The housekeeper takes one look at Roisin and says, 'Oh, it's been that kind of night, has it?'

After a very strong coffee on top of paracetamols, Roisin wanders aimlessly around the house, and it is only when she charges her phone and sees she has five missed calls and three texts from James that a pang of guilt rushes through her body like a lightning strike. She looks at herself in the hallway mirror, her unfaithful self. There is no wry smile or salacious savouring from the night before.

'No point in blaming the alcohol,' she says, talking to her own image.

'No other cock has touched my skin or my desire from the moment I gave my body to you, James,' she says, annoyed with her behaviour of the previous night. Roisin moves closer to the mirror, widening her eyes, sighing. One thing she knows for sure, giving herself to another man will not take away the pain and loss she feels in her heart. Roisin has always felt confident that her worldly insight and inner strength will ensure that her heart does not stray, and it will be her head making the decisions and directing her destiny. She is convinced she can no longer be lured by raw seduction and devilish charm.

She reminds herself that if such a perfect match truly desired her, she would need to fight the inner demons threatening her stability, fearing she might melt at the first taste of an illicit affair. To reassure herself, she always keeps her fingers crossed, figuratively speaking. She is mindful that it's a head, heart, loins thing – a fragile balance with many a tipping point. Roisin, after thirteen years in a relationship, her longest period of commitment by far, feels her loyalties are now divided. She needs to put herself first, above all those that are close to her.

Roisin knows her reactions well, and if she is rejected and discarded, she will not beg for change or plead for exclusivity. She never wants to own someone, or cry for their love; instead, she will quickly look to another horizon. She has never aspired to perfection or pious behaviour; she accepts the weaknesses, the recklessness and the failings of human nature. She knows she has all these traits, and that loyalty takes hard work and self-sacrifice, but loyalty must be a two-way thing. Roisin knows she is sensitive to the intricacies of her marriage, and time is slipping away. James will be here soon, but she feels it is a process she must follow through. When she thinks about the time and effort she has invested in her relationship with James, dismissing the emotion, what's left is transactional, and much more complex. She wonders how you can weigh up the value one put into a relationship, versus the transgressions; the moments when all is given against those, when all is forgotten; the times when you would die for your love, against the times when a week away feels like a much-needed escape, a saving of your sanity.

She remembers good times, the fun, and the meeting of minds. She wonders what she should do with all that stuff, all those years of togetherness. She knows it will always be there, taunting her, reminding her of what she has thrown away. The walk around Monaco hand in hand; the week on the Hebridean Princess, lording it up on what was once Queen Elizabeth's holiday ship; the private jets flying into Courchevel and Austria for the mountain ski holidays. And the simpler things in life, like watching a film together while sharing a box of chocolates, walking the dogs on a summer's day, listening to his stories, his bad jokes and nudging him in the right direction when things went a little off course. Roisin lets out a deep sigh and walks out into the garden in the hope that the fresh air will help clear her head.

James calls her on her mobile.

'Hi. I see you were in Mayfair last night, with Vivi, at a guess.'

'Yes, and with Arrabella,' Roisin replies, giving nothing away.

'So, did you pull?' James sounds disgruntled.

'And if I did, would it have bothered you?' Roisin throws back at him, equally disgruntled.

'Like that, is it?' James replies sarcastically. 'See you when I get home then.'

Clearly unimpressed with the tone in Roisin's voice, he puts the phone down.

'What a front he has! How dare he admonish me?' she thinks, no longer feeling unfaithful, just betrayed.

As the day rolls on, she doesn't want to eat, and she is unable to think straight. There's no escaping the lies, or the truth of where they are: his adultery, her unfaithfulness and where they are heading. She pours herself a Hendrick's and tonic, and sits staring at her dining-room sideboard, facing a perfect display of family photos, positioned artistically so each can be seen. She ponders the fact that in all the years she has been with James, despite her past indiscretions, she feels she has given her everything – their lives together always came first. She looks at Elof, James's grandson by Gabriel his first-born son and his wife Freja. He looks so grown up and handsome in his school uniform. His curious blue eyes, funky blond hairstyle, and cheeky smile are endearing.

Roisin chuckles to herself as she thinks of James calling the gangly, long-limbed thirteen-year-old 'the Viking'. He is his parents' pride and joy, and James's all-time favourite guy. Roisin knows she will never see Elof if she leaves James and the thought of that breaks her heart. She thinks back to the moment when, at fourteen months old, Elof slept in the bed between James and herself when he stayed over for the night. The memory is etched in her mind.

His smell, his touch, his little wriggly body and flailing limbs at first light. She turned her face towards him and never slept a wink, feeling protective and waiting for a moment of gurgling and when his eyes opened to meet hers. Roisin closes her eyes, remembering the feeling and his baby scent as she gently rubbed her nose against his face. This was the closest she had been to motherhood. It was overwhelming in a beautiful and unforgettable way.

And there is Henrika, Elof's younger sister, proudly posing in her school uniform, appearing as sweet as sugar, a mere illusion. Roisin loves her feistiness, her imaginative storytelling and she so wants to be around to see what choices Henrika makes on the journey ahead of her.

There are photos, too, of Ethan and Noah, looking smart and cute when they were very young and in private school; and Orla's girls, Annie and Jemma, in their university caps and gowns with their parents standing proudly by their sides. Roisin is pleased that all the children in her photos have opportunities and good parents who love them very much. With the last swig of Hendrick's, she thinks that if one of them had been her child, then no one could take them away from her. And if they had been her child, she could not leave them. But they are not her children; they belong to James. She remembers, when she was a child, being left alone, unprotected and free to roam the streets where she came to harm.

14

HE WHO WOULD VALIANT BE

Roisin's mood takes a darker turn as she thinks of losing everything she has ever wanted and worked hard for. This feeling is familiar and reminiscent of the time she lost her baby and left Andreas. During her life, there have been many times when sadness brought up the negativity and pain from her past. She doesn't know why this happens, if it is wallowing in self-pity and punishment, or just her emotions getting the better of her. Roisin remembers standing outside a row of council concrete garages in the pouring rain in the autumn of 1976. The metal roll-up doors all looked the same but for different knocks and scratches, and the type of litter that has accumulated in the corners and drains. She looks for a number. Casey, a friend from school, told her to go to number 9. She said she would be there at the end of school; she said she was meeting her boyfriend Errol for a fag and a snog. Roisin was soaked through and was so cold. She banged hard on a garage door, but there was no response. Suddenly, she heard the grinding, clanking sound of metal scraping against metal behind her, as a garage door lifted enough for her to see Casey's head peeking out from underneath.

'Roisin, come in,' she called.

Roisin bowed down enough to clear her body under the garage door. Immediately she was struck by the musty damp and burning smells in the garage. Once her eyes had adjusted to the haze of the flickering candles and smoke that filled the air, she saw how many faces were turned towards her. Six figures, some standing in front of the drab and gloomy walls, others lying on the old mattresses on the floor. The only girl was Casey, the other five were boys, two wearing Moat Boys School uniforms, and three of them who looked older – she had never seen them before. Casey put her arm around the shoulder of one of the older boys and took the cigarette from between his fingers and began to smoke it herself.

'This is my boyfriend, Errol,' she said, looking at Roisin while blowing smoke at the side of his face. Errol stared at her, screwing up his lip. He snatched the cigarette out of her hand. 'Gimme that and suck my dick,' he said to her, grabbing hold of his crotch. The other boys, grabbing their own crotches, whooped and screeched with laughter. Three of the boys started to stare at Roisin. She began to feel uneasy, realising that she was trapped and there was no quick way out. The mood soon became dark. Errol stood next to her and put his hand on her shoulder, placing a joint in between her lips. 'Take a drag,' he insisted, the whites of his eyes brighter as his face moved closer to hers.

She coughed away the smoke, sat on the mattress, and watched as the other boys took it in turns to smoke the joint. Errol lay on top of Casey; her legs were spread out either side of him. Roisin started to feel heady with the smoke, the smells and the creeping fear. The other boys were grinning, nodding their heads, flicking their wrists, shouting, 'Yeah, man. Get them pussy. Go, Errol man.' Laughing as they watched him pull down his jeans, bare his buttocks and pump away on top of Casey. She never made a sound. Roisin tried to stand up, knowing she needed to get the door open and run. Before she could get her footing, the other boys were dragging her back and onto the mattress. The older one straddled her forcibly, pinning her down by her shoulders. She felt hands pulling at her, sitting on her legs, pulling her knickers down and away from her body.

She shouted, 'No, stop! Please stop.' The older boy grabbed her hands and lay on her chest covering her mouth with his, slobbering his spit and tongue in and out of her, and over her face. The smell and feel of him was disgusting. She could not move from under him.

The hands of the other boys were grabbing her between her legs, sticking their fingers into her. The older boy lifted himself from off her chest, while another held down her arms over her head. He opened her white school blouse and laughed when he saw her pink spotty bra. He lifted the bra, exposing her breasts. He pulled down the front of his sweatpants and pulled out his cock and began masturbating with one hand and grabbing at her breasts with the other. Roisin feeling numb, turned her head away and stared into the blackness of the wall. Suddenly, a loud clanging noise filled the garage, and the daylight flooded in. The boys jumped up and off Roisin, hiding their cocks away, letting her free. It was Lenny, Errol's older brother.

Seeing her chance to escape while all the boys were distracted, Roisin scrambled off the mattress and charged through the garage door. Holding her blouse together, she ran all the way to the park, not thinking once about Casey. Roisin remembers thinking, all those years ago, when she was only a child, as she hunkered down in the long grass sobbing, that she was relieved only the boys' fingers had been inside of her. As she closes her eyes, she is taken back to the stench, the sweat and the horror of entrapment, and the black smoke-filled garage that left her choking. Only now, she thinks of Casey, that poor girl, not knowing what became of her. Roisin now finds it difficult to understand why she did not ask at school where Casey was, or why no one ever mentioned her name again.

Even after managing to escape, Roisin was left distraught for weeks, unable to forget the fear she had felt, believing that she was going to be hurt or even killed. And afterwards, how afraid she was that someone would come to know what had happened to her and Casey. It was only school that saved her.

Roisin remembers loving everything about Moat Girls School. It was her sanctuary. Each day, she would look forward to the pomp and ceremony of the weekly morning assembly. On Friday, she would stand in line among the rows of girls dressed in white blouses, red ties, navy skirts, and blazers with the school shield embroidered on the breast pocket. Hands neatly placed by their sides, heads facing forwards, like a parade of soldiers in formation awaiting inspection.

She remembers tittering with her friends about the headmistress, Mrs Rundall – an exceptionally large lady, very much larger around her hips than her upper half. Roisin imagined you could place a plate of chips on those hips, and it would stay put as she wibbled and wobbled, like a huge Weeble, down the long aisle to the lectern standing on the stage, from where she would deliver her morning address to her obedient audience. She remembers her favourite part came at the end of Mrs Rundall's address when she got to raise her eyes up to the majestic arched ceiling and breathe in its majesty. Feeling uplifted, she bellowed out the words, 'He who would valiant be 'gainst all disaster, let him in constancy follow the master.' She was never so full of life as when all around her were singing as one family and the echo of hearty voices eclipsed the banal.

Roisin remembers how she so loved attending art class and how her teacher, whom she admired, encouraged her to go to college and become an art teacher. But she also remembers how little focus she had for academia. She picks up a photo which reminds her how skinny she was, her spindly mottled legs and messy hair. She was never shown as a child how to make the best of herself, with pretty hairstyles, dresses and bows. Roisin smiles to herself, knowing that now, she would never dare leave the house without her lipstick and mascara on. She thinks back to the proudest moment of her school days, when she was coming to the end of her time at Moat School, and Mrs Allen, the head of drama, must have seen something in her that she had no clue was there.

She gave her the task of producing and directing a Christmas play for House Nightingale. They would be competing for the best play in the school, against three other houses, Coutts, Lovelace and Pankhurst, all named after influential women in history and an integral part of Moat Girls School's inspiration for motivation. Roisin threw herself into the project, staying long after school had ended to create, plan and rehearse as much as possible.

She called the play 'Another Brick in the Wall,' a spoof of their rebellious classroom antics and a mickey-take of a few 'odd' teachers. The culmination was the full cast on the stage and all those assembled in the great hall singing Pink Floyd's hit of the same name, which at the time was seen as an anti-establishment, rebellious song and had already been banned in South Africa. Roisin recalls receiving a standing ovation; she had been valiant, and it changed her life. Roisin feels thankful for her school days. Her focus on studying gave her more than just purpose at the time; it breathed life into her latent heart and lay down the foundations of her quest for knowledge and desire to work hard to make a better life for herself.

15

FAITH, A CONTENTED TORTURE

There was never a time when Roisin did not have questions or a puzzle in her head that needed completing. She cared about the bigger picture, where the most interesting questions came from different sources, each offering differing answers, all claiming to be the truth. Questions such as: Why are we here? Where do we come from? Where did the animals originate from? What happens when we die? Roisin remembers reading Anne Frank's diary at a young age, she was a year younger than the author – she has never been able to forget the terrible circumstances in which she died.

At the same time, a darker, further reaching question began to emerge, as she developed a morbid fascination with humankind's ability to inflict pain and torture on the weak, and the vulnerable. In religious knowledge at school, she remembers being taught that eighty per cent of humankind believe there is a God, whom they worship and give thanks to for saving them. But Roisin questioned their loyalty, and wondered how he was saving them, when they all suffered and died.

Her mind could not rest. She questioned why the God of the Jews, Yahweh, let the Nazis murder Anne Frank and six million people, when they worshiped him so fervently. She demanded to know; she wanted answers. When Adanna, a friend from school, gave her a Bible and told her that all the answers she needed were written in this little book, she took it with both hands.

Adanna would walk with Roisin in the park, and they would find a quiet place to study the Bible together. Roisin loved how calm and dignified her friend was and that she never swore or bullied others, like most girls did. Adanna talked about her mother, father and her younger brother Stephen, and how they would sing together twice a week at their place of worship. 'We are one big happy family,' she would say. That was the one thing Roisin desired more than anything for herself, Darra and Orla.

Adanna was delighted to see Roisin standing outside the House of Worship. She proudly introduced each member of her family. Roisin, feeling nervous, thought they all looked so smartly dressed. Adanna linked arms with Roisin and insisted she sit next to her. On entering the building, Roisin was surprised by its simplicity, its lack of statues or cross staring down on the congregation. The red carpet throughout the hall felt as warm and inviting as the people that stood mingling on or walking over it.

Roisin took a slow walk home. There was an explosion of thoughts racing around in her head. She had never felt this way before. So many people wanting to say hello to her, so many interested in who she was and what she was thinking, and everyone hoping they would see her again.

So much about the last two hours had shown her that what went on at her home, within her family, was wrong and needed to stop. Roisin kept her visits to the House of Worship quiet. She dared not tell Darra and Orla for fear of their father finding out. There was no telling how he would react, having been brought up a Catholic. As she delved deeper into theology, she became driven by belief and the love of worship. She ignored the niggling doubt in her heart that told her that surrendering herself and utterly committing herself, which she knew was a requirement to continue enjoying the benefits of her newly found family, would bring with it a huge challenge.

Roisin thinks back to who she was then and finds it hard to believe that she committed her whole being to a life of faith and chastity. In many ways, she remembers feeling free of the trappings of worldliness and the demands of self-gratification, and the more she studied, the more she wanted to be part of the fold, and the brighter her life became. She became a dogged believer and, in her initial spiritual awakening, set her sights on becoming a missionary. She recalls a deep satisfaction and contentment within herself, one that she later found so hard to keep, and a sense that nothing she had done since had given her the same feeling. Even though her present life could not be more opposite, and she wonders to herself how different her life would have been if her faith had been strong enough, maybe she would have found a loving husband and together they would have gone on to save the world, she feels humbled and privileged to have experienced what having faith really means to her and how it shaped her views.

Adanna's parents were aware of Roisin's living arrangements with Ciara and her drunken father, and the fact that going home was not an option for her. They suggested that she moved in with an elder and his wife who had no children of their own. Looking back at this time in her life, Roisin feels that living with a couple of the same faith ultimately changed her life's direction, giving her the space and stability to mature and take her studies at school seriously.

Her dark emotions lifted, and she found her voice, her humour and the young woman she was always meant to be. Although she now feels she had to grow up far too early. She senses her worldliness is apparent to others, in her watchful gaze, curiosities and serious words, more common in those of age and wisdom, which reveal her need for more than just paternal affection.

Roisin now recognises that finding solace within religion at that time may have been a means of escape from her father and can see that its knowledge emboldened her to become the woman she is now. But the decisions she made, as a teenage girl, with the man whom she came to live with, very nearly brought on her demise. After eight months of cohabitating with Master elder Richard Danby and his wife, Corrine, playful paternal pillow fights became sinful groping romping sessions that ended in fornication. Tricky Dicky, as Roisin later called him, wept with regret only once, and only when penetration had come to an end.

Roisin remembers clearly the day when the impact of what she had done hit her for the first time. She was sitting by herself among thousands of people at a religious convention in a stadium in Dudley. The words on the pamphlet jumped out at her, boring into her eyes, showing their displeasure, screaming at her: 'Adultery, sex before marriage and keeping oneself pure for the Lord in an ungodly world'.

'That's me,' Roisin thought to herself. 'Me and Richard.' Roisin remembers how wretched she felt, believing that her God was watching her keep up the pretence of being righteous and without sin as she walked and talked, sermonising from door to door with her guilt-ridden mouth, the same mouth that kissed the lips and the body that did not belong to her, corrupting what was good. The pangs of guilt she had tried so hard to suppress surged violently to the surface. Her face became hot and flushed, her heart pounding in her chest. Roisin recalls having to cover her mouth to contain her stomach contents as she ran past those already seated and down the concrete steps towards the toilets – as she saw Richard Danby take to the podium and begin shuffling his notes.

When her stomach had nothing left to give, she sat on the toilet seat with her head in her hands and thought of Richard, wondering if he felt the same as she did – unable to pray, or look at himself in the mirror because of their deceitfulness. Now the wrongs they committed are a lifetime ago, Roisin feels able to reflect more clearly on how Richard was able to stand there and preach to thousands of people about temperance and chastity. He may have thought he would lose everything because of what he had done. Everyone hides their secrets for fear of grave consequences. Just as James is doing.

Roisin drifts back to her memories of the stadium, of her sitting on the toilet, rubbing away her streaming tears, trying to recall why and how her relationship with Richard had taken a sinister turn. Richard and Corrine were such a nice couple. They gave her all their attention and it didn't take long for Roisin to develop a strong bond and a need to be close to them. Roisin would sit on a soft red chair on the front row of the congregation, with an open Bible on her lap, looking up at Richard standing on the podium tending to his flock, and he became her hero. In the evenings, she would sit next to him on the settee and see the warm and sweet-natured man that he was. Corrine did not like to cook, so Roisin became his helper in the kitchen, helping to prepare their evening meals. She would travel on the back of his motorbike for long rides to Bradgate Park. Corrine did not like the motorbike.

One sunny Saturday morning, while lying on the grass next to each other, with their legs and hands sprawled over the same blades of grass, sharing the same hue and taste of nature, she felt a shifting of her feelings. She was leaving childish thoughts behind and beginning to think like a young woman. She was seeing Richard less as a tutor and more as a lover. Months of togetherness, overlooked or disregarded as innocent by Corrine and others, allowed fondness to mature into inappropriate affection and a longing to touch the other unclothed and in ways they should not. Richard and Corrine did not sleep in the same bedroom, so he was free to be with Roisin, staying up late into the night, sitting close to her on the settee, her leg often wrapped over his, his arm over her shoulder, her head on his chest.

Their behaviour was all ambiguous until one Friday evening when Corrine was having a bath, Richard wrapped both hands around Roisin's face, pulling her close to him. He kissed her full on the lips, his mouth opening and pressing into hers. Moving slowly and passionately, she could feel his chest bellowing in and out next to hers. Roisin put her hands under his jacket and around his back, encouraging the drive of his body into hers. His lips reluctantly left hers.

'I love you,' he said. 'I'm sorry, but I love you.'

'I love you too, and I'm not sorry,' Roisin replied, staring longingly into his eyes. They both walked into the kitchen, with knowing glances, served the food out onto plates and sat with Corrine, all three eating together, mostly in silence.

After replaying this moment of herself as a young girl, Roisin sees her actions as calculating and self-serving. Despite her young years, she knew what was right and what was wrong. Even her faith did not stand in the way of her getting what she wanted: attention and love. From that first kiss came a flurry of snatched moments of touching and grasping over clothed bodies. Of simulated foreplay, with her straddling him on the settee as he guided her dressed body up and down over the crest of his hardening cock, his eagerness and pleasure stirring her on to move more intuitively. They always stopped at unzipping, undressing and exposing the flesh. This helped them keep up the pretence. He went to work as a draughtsman, she went to school as a fifteen-year-old, and both went to their place of worship as faithful servants.

They sought out time when they could be alone together in the house to secure undisturbed, stolen moments when they were free to further their desires. Not more than a month after that first kiss, she had his cock in her hand and she pleasured him with her strokes, with her beauty and her willingness. His hands weaved through and under her clothing, finding her moistness, her young and virginal place. He delighted in being the first to touch her softness with love and fulfil her feminine desires. With his coaching, she learnt how to keep this their secret. She knew how to turn her head away from him when she felt herself staring at him in company and restrain herself from reaching out to him with an affectionate touch or rushing to sit next to him, unless they were at home alone.

Roisin thinks about how the deception, the lies and their selfish acts took over her day-to-day thoughts, not the thoughts a fifteen-year-old should be focused on. She blames herself for her eagerness to take what was not hers to take. But now, as an older woman, she knows Richard took advantage of an infatuated teenager. He abused her when he should have walked away. After Corinne and Roisin spent a weekend together alone while Richard was at an elders' convention in New York, Roisin began to feel the weight of their deception on her shoulders. She asked Corrine why they did not sleep in the same bed and why she never saw them kiss or cuddle. Corrine wrapped her arms around her and told her that these matters were not for her to worry about. Roisin cried tears of guilt, knowing what she had been doing with Corinne's husband over the last seven months behind her back. She decided she needed to talk to Richard, that they needed to stop.

As soon as he walked through the door on his return, he had a coldness about him, only speaking to her to say morning and goodnight. One Friday morning, Corrine told Roisin that she was going to spend a few nights at her mother's house in Sheffield, something she did a few times a year. Roisin returned home early that afternoon from school to find Richard crying into his hands.

Roisin thinks about this moment, searching for clarity. Why did she see it as her place to comfort him? She can only conclude that this was something she had been doing most of her young life, comforting her brother and sister. It became a natural response to nurture, to be the grown-up. She threw her school bag on the floor and lay her arm across Richard's shoulders. He looked up at her. He must have been crying a lot, she thought, for his eyes to be that red and swollen.

'Hello, you, the trouble in my heart,' he said, as he wiped away the tears on his face and chin. 'What a mess I am,' he said, turning himself around, facing her, reaching for her hand, the distance and coldness now dissipated. 'I'm sorry for ruining your life. I had no right to touch you. I have no right to want you, to need you.'

Roisin, without thinking, sat on his lap and wrapped her arms around him, squeezing him close to her. They sat there together, entwined, with their heads on each other's shoulders, for what seemed to Roisin to be a very long time. Later that evening they cooked together for the first time in a long while. They smiled and laughed and played cards.

As the night drew in, they began to glance at the clock and share a knowing look that it would soon be time to say goodnight. They stood together at the bottom of the stairs, and he kissed the crown of her head. 'Go to bed, to your bed, and go to sleep,' he told her firmly.

She listened to the sound of his heavy footsteps ascending the wooden steps and on the wooden floorboards along the long corridor to the bedroom at the end of the house, the bedroom furthest away from hers. She stood at the bottom of the stairs for a few minutes, her stomach churning, her mind restless, her need to be close to him rising, reciting the 'what ifs' in her head, her restless heart running away with the moment. She walked slowly up the stairs. Reaching the top, she peered towards his bedroom. The door was open. She went into their shared bathroom, washed, brushed her teeth and combed her hair, all the while wondering if Richard lay awake, thinking of her. Wrapped in a towel, she paused outside the bathroom door, before turning and walking towards her own bedroom. She slipped on her blush-pink nightie and slid between the sheets. She left her door open.

'Goodnight, Richard,' she said, a moment later. He told her to go to sleep, his voice carrying with it an echo down the long sparse corridor. An hour later she still couldn't sleep. She threw back the covers and sat on the edge of the bed. 'What if,' she repeated to herself. She walked out of her bedroom, down the long corridor and into Richard's bedroom. Now she is older and thinking about the moment before James was unfaithful to her, she wonders if she entered his mind, or was he, too, able to discard any thought of the one he would hurt and the consequences, just as she did with Corrine. Roisin remembers how driven she was to be close to Richard and she now feels her actions at this time were more about sex and wanting more of him than love. She could, at this point, have denied her need, but she alone, knowingly, selfishly took what she wanted.

Richard lay there wide awake. He turned his face towards her, and he lifted the corner of the covers, inviting her into his bed. She rolled on top of his naked body. His hands ran eagerly down both sides of her body, moving effortlessly over the sheerness of her nightwear and onto the bare cheeks of her pert bottom, lifting and pushing her into his groin.

'I have seen this negligee many times blowing dry on the line, in the breeze with the sun's rays darting through it … And all I imagined was you wearing it, and your naked body, tempting me and begging me to look.'

They kissed passionately, their mouths open, their tongues free to give and take, her breasts riding up and down his chest, as his movements became more forceful and urgent. She wanted to hold his cock as she had done so many times before. She flipped her body over, facing his hard on, and with the technique he had shown her, proceeded to work him slowly. Richard slipped off the straps on her nightwear and grasped both her breasts in his hands. She leant forward and began using her tongue, licking the top of him, and up and down his shaft.

'I haven't done this before,' he said, his voice breaking and breathy, his legs shaking.

'Neither have I,' Roisin replied, before taking him into her mouth.

'Oh God, oh God,' Richard murmured, in pleasure and surprise.

Suddenly, in a frantic move, he grabbed hold of her around the waist and threw her down onto her back, forcing her legs apart. He rammed his brute into her, causing her to gasp at the pain. He held her fast about her shoulders, no longer gentle, no longer thinking of her. He thrust into her until his last, and dropped onto her body, his head facing down until his breathing calmed. The realisation of what he had just done only then hitting him hard. He rolled off her without saying a word or giving her a look. He sat on the edge of the bed and ran his fingers through his hair. He stood up and he went into the bathroom and closed the door.

Roisin remembers this moment too well. It made her feel like she had when she was trapped in the dark and damp garage, afraid, held down and physically in pain. She was left feeling stunned. There was no tenderness, no words of love. The moment felt brutal, her control taken away from her. She knew she was out of her depth. Roisin lay on Richard's bed, noticing her nightie was ripped. She pulled her knees up to her chest. She felt ashamed and surprised about the way things had gone. She had not expected to feel so much pain or for Richard to walk away the way he had.

She got off the bed sheepishly and went to knock on the bathroom door, but she stopped after hearing him whimper. She put her dressing gown on and went downstairs for a drink. Richard appeared in the kitchen. 'We need to talk,' he said in a harsh tone. He asked her with an air of ruthlessness if she had periods and, if so, when was her last.

To his annoyance, she was slow to answer and then failed to remember. 'This ends now,' he stated. 'I am a man of God; a married man and you are a child.' He made her promise not to say a word to anyone.

Roisin thinks back to those months, keeping their dirty secret. It was both exciting and, at times, a heavy burden to carry alone. She bragged about a secret boyfriend she had to her school friends, boasting about losing her virginity, lapping up the attention.

Many months later, and a few days after the convention, Roisin knocked on his office door.

'A cup of tea, Richard. Here, for you,' she said and gave it to him with a smile.

'Oh, thank you, Roisin,' he said. 'You can always read my mind. I'm so pleased we can still be such close friends.'

Richard and Roisin embraced and instinctively, without thinking, kissed each other on the lips, just as Mrs Maynard from the congregation banged on the window. Richard, startled, jumped up and opened the door. 'I came to see Corrine, Richard, but see you are distracted in the worst possible way. I trust you will contact elder Vernon before I do.' She left with a cloud of disgust hanging over her head. Richard looked at Roisin and let out a long sigh.

'I need to make a phone call … You will be OK,' he said, nodding his head. Roisin remembers at the time thinking she had no idea what 'You will be OK' meant. What followed was humiliating and traumatic, and she was not OK.

She remembers sitting in the front row of the House of Worship, shaking, while her sins were publicly announced to everyone present. This was after she had attended a meeting with four elders who each took their turn to deliver their reproach, naming Roisin as 'Jezebel, the Devil's companion, she who riotously disrupted a loyal servant restraining loins, breaking his resolve to remain faithful to his wife and to God.' And stating that 'for the enticing and seduction of one of their devout and finest, the Jezebel must be cast out.' Richard was stripped of his eldership but stayed within the fold and his marriage survived.

Even today, Roisin can still see the faces of the elders. All old men, talking over her and asking the most personal of questions. At the time of the meeting, she was feeling ashamed and embarrassed, but later, when she was made to feel dirty and was ostracised by most of the congregation, she saw herself as harshly judged, and turned her back on her accusers. She was angry and hurt and was no longer seeking forgiveness. Her young life was left in disarray, Now cast adrift with lacerating guilt. She saw herself as too bad to be righteous, and too damaged to live in the real world. Her faith, once her sanctuary and now the voice of reason. Her heart still belongs to God, a contentment with which she had found peace, but now she was tortured with self-loathing and the loss of those whom she had come to know as family. Roisin moved out of Richard and Corrine's home and moved into a bedsit. Corrine visited her a few months after she had left and told her they were leaving England at the end of the month and starting a new life in New Zealand. She told Roisin that she, too, was at fault and that they all needed to forgive each other. Roisin may have accepted at that time, that the loneliness and pain she felt was deserved for her part in going to Richard's bed and urging him to take her virginity – but now she sees that Richard, a much older man in a position of power and influence, took advantage of a vulnerable girl.

16

THE CHURCH BELLS

The present, Sunday, 1 p.m.

Jax and Coco sit obediently looking up at their mistress, awaiting her command for a paw, the signal that brings the pieces of chicken out of her fingers and into their mouths. The patio doors are open, letting the freshness of the outside in. Roisin can hear the distant ringing of the village church bells and wonders what they are celebrating – a service, a special historical day or maybe a wedding. There will be singing no doubt, and everyone will be wearing their Sunday best, and wearing the best of themselves, their kindness, their open and willing hearts, embracing and sharing the burdens of life.

These are the parts about sharing a faith she misses from her past, and always will. She looks up at the beautiful big blue sky, hoping to find a connection, a link with God, just to have a chat, a few words about her mess-up and how sorry she is. 'God, I know I was only fifteen, but the way I remember it, I knew right from wrong. I don't remember how it felt at that time when I was so selfish, so blinkered that only my feelings and needs mattered. Corrine was never in my thoughts when I touched her husband, in her house. I was so callous and deceitful. How could I have done that to someone who took me in and cared for me? Was I so broken that getting fixed clouded all my sensibilities?'

'Was my longing for love and to be noticed and heard so gripping that I orchestrated my own story by acting out my vulnerabilities, and the very same play performed by Laurette and all the women who twinkled at strange men on the streets? It was not so much love I was searching for, but a protector, a saviour, within whose arms I could feel safe ... and maybe loved. I am sorry, dear Father, that you were not enough. Now I am dyeing the grey, and the extra weight I am carrying is straining every sinew, and the strength of my heart is weakened, my perspective I feel is that of a broader church.' Roisin feels her inclination to desperately cling onto the gates of heaven left her many years ago, and her need to worship with others is no longer present, but in moments like this, her God comes back into life, and a two-way conversation once again ensues.

'Why not save everyone? Is not the God I read of in the Old Testament and the Torah the same God in the Koran? ... all people who look to the heavens or have faith of any kind are looking for you. Your light flickers and darkens and is difficult to follow. The path is unclear, the terms are untenable ... The God of the Old Testament is a god of war, and of war there is already too much on Earth. You are still there, tearing at my heartstrings, and in equal measures leaving me fearful. I listen, and I watch as the world stumbles on, and with the rest of humankind, I will see what your day will bring.'

Roisin, seeking closure from this difficult memory, writes a poem to her God and once again shuts away his voice.

Nothing Here to Save

How I reached this instance, I have yet to realise
For I have become two people existing in one space
The shadows overhead mingle and merge, dulling
    sunrise
The good and the evil, a war, for which I have no taste
A coldness where physical and spiritual forbade an
    embrace
I see no peace in the depths, only a joyless pretence
My strength has failed me, nothing left here to save
You gave family, you gave purpose, a voice that
    became mine
But the darkness weighed heavy and blackened my way
As so many before, and so many to come, I am not of
    the meek
And so it is that before you I stand, and the truth in
    my heart I betray.

Roisin, 2023

. . .

Sitting alone in her bedsit, Roisin could hear coughing and retching in the mornings, and sometimes through the night. It sounded like old men, hacking up from smoker's lungs. She was afraid to tell a teacher where she lived because she was certain they would contact social services and she would be sent back to her father's house. She would soon be sixteen and thought no one could then tell her what to do.

Richard had paid her rent in advance for six months only – her landlord gave her two weeks' notice after failing to continue the payments. Orla had mentioned that Dad wanted her to come to Ireland with them, and he had said she should live with Aunt Maeve and Uncle Niall. Roisin had other ideas. She wanted to go to college and become an art teacher. The last thing she wanted was to go and live with another witch. She knew of a local homeless refuge for girls and women, because Richard had mentioned it as an option. She knew this was now her only choice and so she arranged a meeting with the owners.

Roisin wandered around the Haymarket Shopping Centre, enquiring after a job in the same place where Ciara and she had stolen their monkey boots. That seemed a long time ago. And she looked so different now, which she thought was a good thing as it meant she would not be recognised as the thieving scallywag she once was. Roisin remembers walking into Van Allen Fashions. She was ill prepared, unfashionable and expected to be rebuffed, but the manager, Mrs Roberts, gave her a second look.

'Tell me why you would like to work here, young lady,' she said with a warm and widening smile. Roisin recalls stumbling with her words, and saying how much she loved art, and that she would love to create a good display in her windows with the mannequins, and that she was a good listener and learnt fast. 'Oh, good. You sound just like what we need. Shall we look at you working on Saturdays first and see how you get on?' Mrs Roberts said, leaning towards Roisin with her very made-up face – lots of shiny eyeshadow and bright red lipstick that went over the edges. Roisin could not help but stare at her perfectly coiffed hair that made her look like a big, soft Chow Chow dog. She reminded Roisin of Mrs Muggleton and all her loveliness. There were two other older ladies who worked at Van Allen, and Mrs Roberts' daughter Jilly, who worked on the Biba makeup section. They all mothered Roisin. It was her dream job, and she was happy again.

It didn't matter that she was living in a homeless place. Mrs Roberts knew, and she still wanted her. After Roisin had finished at Moat Girls School, it joined with the Boys School to become Moat Community College. She had won the competition to create a picture that signified the transition and was invited to attend the celebrations.

On the morning of the open day, Jilly, armed with her Biba makeup and hairdryer, gave Roisin a stunning makeover. Her bright green eyes stood out against the black spidery mascara and dark brown kohl eye pencil, her subtle red lip liner and glossy lipstick accentuated her pout, and her long auburn hair bounced vivaciously over her shoulders, with its fringe lifting off her face, flicked back on either side, framing her new womanly look. The ladies at Van Allen dressed her in a fine wool, Air Force blue, long pencil-skirt suit that tapered in at the waist. She wore her first pair of American tan tights and patent black court shoes and finished off the look with a black clutch bag, complete with her very own lipstick.

'I wonder if Mr Carrington is still there,' she mused, with her hands sat on her hips, twirling in front of the tall, long mirror. She was amazed by how she looked. She thought herself beautiful. She let out a churlish chuckle. 'Wait until you see me now, sir,' she thought, flicking her head back and ruffling her curls as she closed the glass entrance door of the fashion shop, throwing a final glance back at the ladies waving her good luck. Feeling proud, she lifted her chin, took in the rush of cool fresh air, and with a confident stride, managed to catch the number 39 bus heading out of Highfields and towards Moat Community College and her mission. Her mission – to find another much older man to lavish her misguided affections upon, something at the time she knew she was doing, but didn't understand why.

Now she is in her late fifties, Roisin knows why it was always an older man that turned her head. She always thought that experience and insight came with age, and she needed to look up to the man she was with. But she has come to realise over time that this is not always the case. She would have admired a partner of her own age, if the right man had come her way.

17

THE MAD AND THE BAD

Leicester, 1980

The small, dimly lit office was quite unremarkable. A plain wooden desk only big enough to accommodate one chair sat positioned next to a small sash window, allowing just enough light to stream in to allow you to read the paperwork, if you held it at a certain angle. There were a few framed certificates grouped together on the opposite wall, but the print was too small for Roisin to read from where she was sitting on a not-so-comfortable square wooden chair with no arm supports – a bit like the ones she remembered sitting on at school, she thought. There was a second school chair tucked in the corner of the room. There was nothing of interest lying around on the desktop for her to nosy over to keep her occupied while she sat waiting for Mr and Mrs Vickers to enter the room and determine if she was the kind of individual that they would want to live in their homeless refuge.

Mr Vickers, a retired Parish Councillor, and his wife, Carol, were both avid churchgoers and prided themselves on taking in the waifs and strays and giving them sanctuary and a direction in life. At least, that's what they told her while the three of them shared a plate of biscuits and a pot of tea. Even after delivering the house rules in unison and in a very authoritarian manner, Roisin still saw them as nice people doing good deeds, but she sensed they were no pushovers. She listened carefully: two strikes and you're out. Roisin listened intently to Carol's sickly sweet, but firm voice, telling her about her Christian values and how she needed to abide by them. Little did Carol know that Roisin knew all about conforming to Christian values, something she now preferred to keep to herself.

Roisin noticed the list of rules plastered on the kitchen wall: 'No boys, no alcohol, no smoking, no swearing and no loud noises in the house after nine o'clock.' Roisin was saddened to be homeless. She thought herself to be kind and giving, she didn't drink or behave badly and now she was afraid others would assume that she did. Roisin, demonstrating her best behaviour, gracefully accepted the key to her bedroom door. The twelve-bedroomed Victorian house had been divided into two partitioned living areas, each with their own entrance, garden space, six bedrooms, a small kitchen, dining area and a living room. One side housed mature ladies and the other, those between the age of sixteen and twenty-five.

Roisin had to spend the first three months in the 'old lady' section until a room became vacant on the other side. It was not until she walked into the bedroom and noticed there were two beds that she realised she would have to share with someone else. She figured she had no choice.

She would stay at the refuge for a few weeks, find more work and eventually move into her own flat. She was still living in there fourteen months later.

On the morning after her first night's stay, she was awoken by a jolly and loud Carol, storming through her bedroom door with a walking stick in her hand. She proceeded to prod Roisin in the bum as soon as she saw her dive under the bedcovers.

'Wakey, wakey, rise and shine, madam. It's seven o'clock. Time to get up and smell the daffodils,' she said, with a last vigorous dig of her stick before moving onto the next victim.

Carol took great delight in her duties, as she called them, every morning, except Sunday, when she left her house early to be at church. She pontificated and extolled the virtues of seizing the day. She would not adapt her routine, even after she was told that Roisin had started work at Bilberries Nightclub and would not be arriving back at the house until three in the morning. Roisin told quite a few lies to secure her new job: her age, how long she had been working at Van Allen on the tills, pretending she was good at addition and also not mentioning where she lived. She was asked to start the same evening and wear a short skirt and lots of makeup.

'It brings the punters in, having a pretty girl serving them a pint,' said the stuttering barrel-shaped, cigar-smoking manager.

Although, at first, she found her new evening job quite frightening, all that male attention and gutter language, she soon learnt to work the banter to her advantage. She kept her past to herself, and over time, she began to fit in with the streetwise bar girls. She would swear, smoke and flirt with any man that took her fancy. She left no sign of her pious and gentle self. She had her own money and now had the nerve to make her own rules.

The old ladies who lived in the refuge all wore faces that told of stories of hardship and abandonment. Mavis was a short, thick-set lady who would walk for miles all day long around Leicester city centre. The weight of the bags she was carrying, and her bowed knees caused her to rock from side to side. She had her favourite armchair, the one closest to the television and positioned by the bay window from where she would watch the world passing by. She sat with an overflowing ashtray on her lap, and always seemed to be stubbing one out or lighting one up.

Roisin wondered what had happened for Mavis to end up homeless, with not one of her nine children caring for her. She felt nothing but pity for her, thinking it must be worse being left in such a place at her age. Roisin vowed to herself that she must work hard and leave as soon as she had enough money. She always made a point of saying goodbye to Mavis before setting off to work at the nightclub. She has never forgotten the image of her hairy chubby feet, or how her knees and thighs spread outwards, wafting the day's sweat and smells into everyone's breathing space. No one dared tell her to close her legs. Roisin can still hear the words that Mavis would repeat to her over and over in her broad northern accent.

'Ooh, Roisin, ya look like the belle of the ball, you do,' she would say as the smoke escaped between her rotten and gapped teeth.

And Roisin knew she would never forget Angie, in her forties, who was childlike, and shadowed her wherever she went. A few years later after Roisin had left the refuge, Angie saw her standing in a queue in the Yorkshire Bank and she playfully reached for her, tickling her ribs. Roisin, out with her trendy, good-looking friends brushed Angie away abruptly, pretending not to know her. She sniggered along with her friends when they made derogatory comments about how Angie looked and how she spoke. Roisin was too embarrassed to reveal she had lived with Angie, and that they were once close. Immediately after, Roisin felt so ashamed of her actions; the image of Angie walking away wiping her tears away has never left her. Her worst memories from her time at the house were of the times when 'the possessed one', the name she gave to a retired headmistress with whom she had to share her bedroom for a week, sat bolt upright every night in her bed, rocking back and forth, swearing at her as she lay awake petrified. All Roisin could think about was the film *The Exorcist*. Only Mavis was unafraid of the headmistress, who backed away after Mavis threw a full ashtray in her face. Her social worker finally found her a more suitable place, once she was diagnosed with dementia, and after that the house settled down.

Roisin looks back on her young self during this period, reliving some of these awful memories. It seems so surreal that this happened to her, now she is living in the most stunning home and surrounded by such beautiful things. She had to grow up fast, think on her feet and adapt. Once Roisin had moved to the other side of the house, the fun side, where hiding boyfriends, alcohol and smoking from

Carol was all part of the daily entertainment, everything changed for her. Her youthful competitiveness came to the fore. She was the only girl working, the only one with nice clothes, makeup and, by now, a very handsome lover called Ian, whom she was keen to show off.

While Roisin was working at Bilberries Nightclub, one of the other barmaids, Trudie, found herself on the streets after a row with her mother. Roisin asked her to come to the refuge, as her room now had an empty bed and Trudie would get more financial benefits from the government, and as a homeless person, she would also be a priority on the council house waiting list. She remembers the last few months being a lot of fun. Eventually, never having lost sight of her plan, Roisin moved to Nuneaton and Trudie became her lodger. At the refuge, Roisin crossed paths with the bad and the mad, and the downright unbelievable. It wasn't easy living with a bunch of misfits, but she now appreciates that they were unfortunate, mentally ill and desperately in need of help, just like she was at the time.

18

THE SEDUCER

Wrapped in the Devil's Embrace ...

The present, Sunday, 2 p.m.

Deep in thought, Roisin paws over the photo in her hand, one of her drop-dead gorgeous ex-lover Ian Hayden. She runs her finger down the centre of his chest and down to the edge of his vivid blue swim shorts. The image of him, standing tall, posing for his photo on Studland Bay beach in Dorset suddenly comes alive in her hand and in the depths of her. That's all it takes, a hint of his presence, for her mind to cascade through her memory, sinking into a moment emblazoned on her psyche. Its smell and touch coursing through her veins, resurrecting the memories of the beginnings of her sexual education. It is the summer of 1983; Roisin is nineteen.

Roisin sees another photo. This one she remembers Ian taking of her, while she lay posing for him, naked on the bed in their hotel room. She looks sun-kissed and radiant. She remembers how young she was, fresh but not innocent, aware of her alluring demeanour, but not her childlike appeal. Her button nose sprinkled with freckles; full, shapely lips, naturally plump and baby pink, yet bloodied and bitten by Ian amid an insatiable paroxysm of experienced lust. Her gloriously red hair, curls tumbling effortlessly over her breasts, long enough to dance over her areola and around her nipples. Her oval, emerald-green eyes, curious and reaching, free of makeup, natural and lively.

Roisin remembers his face. A flash of his perfectly aligned white teeth framed by a 'Jack the lad', smarmy, one-sided grin – always present, telling of a restless mind brewing wicked intention. Eyes, dark and moody, persuasive, preparing her for the enactment of the next enrapturing. There was no resisting him. She belonged to him – in submission, for him to crush or to cherish as he pleased. He was a burly twenty-five-year-old when their paths merged. His name touches her lips only when reminiscing, and competing with girlfriends over who has relished the most urgent carnal pleasures with the most jaw-dropping Adonis.

Roisin, always keen to present the down-and-dirty juicy bits accompanied by photographic proof of her bragged-about rampant gladiator, proudly savours the 'I told you so' swoons. However, fourteen months of devouring this imperious, physically flawless cocksman, subjugated her sense of self, and set her up for a lifetime of pleasing and wanting the kind of man a good mother would warn her daughter to run from. Roisin's thoughts jump back to James. She is sure a good mother would also dissuade her from dating James, a much older man with two marriages behind him and three older children; or staying with him now, considering how he has treated her. The passion was there for both Ian and James at the beginning, and right now she sees her relationship with James ending as badly as it did with Ian. Ian's assurances convinced Roisin that the first fourteen months of their relationship was exclusive, even though he was married and breaking his wedding vows on the very first day he set eyes on her. Now she knows better; he was incapable of loyalty.

Two weeks before the photo of her naked on the bed was taken, Roisin was alone in a city-centre sauna, on a not-so-reputable street, emptying a ladle of water onto hot coals. Her face and body smarted instantly from the sudden ejected spray of searing steam. Unwrapping a towel slowly from around her body, she placed it beneath her, reducing the heat that was emitting from the wooden slats into her skin. She stretched, exhaling into a contented posture, closing her eyes and for a few moments enjoying the sensations and smells of dripping hot water and healing isolation.

Roisin longed for time and space to reclaim herself. The receptionist had reassured her that she would be alone due to the short time left before closing; she drifted slowly into serene solitude. Her day's work toyed with her mind, leaving her empty and unfulfilled. The banality of factory life with its incessant tedium of revving overlocking and sewing machines, and dreary murmurings from the lines of seated women, heads down, rocking in time with the hum of mechanical noise, numbed her senses.

The intense heat of the sauna jolted her into consciousness, arresting her descent into much-needed sleep. On taking a deep breath, she was suddenly interrupted by the sound of a masculine, guttural clearing of the throat which filled the small wooden cabin, quickening her beating heart. She was now fully alert and aware of her vulnerability and need for self-preservation. Her first instinct was to stay ridged, unaffected. She knew that every part of her was laid bare and exposed to this man, in what suddenly felt like a coffin. His eyes were free to peruse her nakedness.

Her thighs and knees slowly rolled inwards towards each other, her pelvis tilted, pushing into the hard, wooden surface in a vain attempt to keep her private self hidden. She knew he was observing the erratic rise and fall of her exposed breasts, her flaring nostrils, her flickering eyelids. She was demanding her eyes to stay shut but they needed to open; panic began to take hold. Roisin sensed his empowerment, his amusement. Her clasped hands dug harder into the sides of her thighs.

He was waiting for a response. She listened to the hastening rhythm of his breathing. She felt his impatient stare, his wanting to see all of her. Keeping her body still, she tilted her head away from the sauna wall, opening her eyes wide. Her unblinking stare met his. He was sitting opposite her, on the bench, next to the door. His body leaning forward, both hands clasped together, resting on his knees. He spoke.

'Hello, you. You're looking good.' Roisin, still gripped with fear was unable to bring herself to respond. She lay still. Again, the man spoke. 'I am a trained masseuse. Let me massage you. It will be fun.' His words delivered slowly in a deep and husky voice.

His fixed smile stretched from ear to ear, as his gaze rolled freely over her still-naked body. She shifted her eyes to take in more of him. His long black hair, swept off his face, flowed down the back of his neck, reaching his broad and tanned shoulders. As he dropped his head forward he closed his eyes. He suddenly raised both hands, his fingers sweeping through his wet fringe. He looked up to the ceiling, expanding his toned muscular chest in an exaggerated display, his predatory smile unflinching. He was handsome, masculine, commanding in his movements.

His body was powerful, naked and ready to perform. She took in his maleness, the size, the way it hung, noticing the details; the hot water dripping down the shaft as it gently swayed. He checked it out, he looked at her checking him out. Her mind was crashing, her heart was galloping. Her body still naked and still. He started to giggle to himself. 'I won't hurt you. I mean, I want you. You can see that I want you.' He raised his eyebrows, deepening his smile, widening his dark brown eyes, urging her to succumb to what he was offering.

Roisin regained her courage, sitting up quickly in a single move. She grabbed her towel from under her body and draped it in between her breasts. Squeezing her arms together, she stood tall, keeping her eyes fixed on his.

'I must leave now,' she stated in a firm and assertive manner. He held her stare. 'You are too close to the door,' she pointed out, her heart pounding faster, her breathing now laboured. He shifted his body across the bench away from the door, his eyes still fixed on hers.

'You are free to go as you please,' he replied calmly. His smile now softened; his desire left still hard. Roisin closed the sauna door behind her.

Taking in a deep breath, she hastened her stride towards the showers. Stepping through the Perspex door she noticed the grime and mould in between the tiles and in the corners of the white ceiling. It felt sordid. The rusting metal dial was hard to turn, and the water slow to reach a passable temperature.

She lifted her head, closing her eyes as the water gushed over her, cooling her body and face. For a moment, she felt relief. Naively, she felt safe. She ran her hands over her face as if wiping away the guilt and emerged feeling powerful. She loved the feeling of her body as it took in the pleasure of him, the excitement, the anticipation of touching and of being touched by this tall, handsome stranger. He was so much more than what had been before. Her naked body wanted him. Roisin found herself smiling at her own thoughts, picturing the man's slightly saturnine features, his strong jaw line, his compelling leer, his eyes demanding she reach out and touch him. His presence so close to her, distressing, yet so thrilling.

She ran her hands slowly down over her breasts, imagining they were his. She turned around and faced the door. Through the waterfall, she saw a blurred outline of his image. 'Who is he?' she cried within. The door opened, he stepped in, closing the door behind him. He picked up the soap and began rolling it in his hands until it lathered. Now he was smiling, towering above her, filling the space, ready to perform. This time, the fear was palpable. There was no way out. Her silence and self-control further excited him. She was no longer free to leave. She was there for the taking.

His hands swept purposefully over her body, mapping out every contour, every groove and hidden space. She pushed herself into the back wall, resisting his efforts. He pushed harder up around the back of her neck, grasping her hair, twisting it in his hands, giving him a stronger hold to lead. Her body was stiff, her hands closed. The sound of the water surging over his back, his groaning and her thundering heart, now a torrent in her head. His movements became slower, his eyes and lips a breath away from hers. He wrapped both arms around her waist, lifting her to her toes, bringing her close to his chest.

'I will stop now and leave if you wish,' he quietly whispered in her ear. The water ran erratically down over his flickering eyelids, pooling in his open mouth. 'Tell me you don't want this,' he teased, penetrating her gaze, searching intently for a response. He loosened his grip; she felt him drawing away. She looked down at the widening gap between their bodies. She no longer felt the shape and heat of his manhood between her legs. A feeling her body pulsated against. Her wanting masked the fear of the unknown, of the threat of him overpowering her and taking her last breath. A stranger who from this moment could leave her dead. Only a few seconds for her to process her thoughts: 'Am I playing with my life? I did not scream, I did not say no. From the first moment I saw you, my eyes did not deceive me, my loins would not deny me. I want you, all of you, whoever you are.'

Roisin had never had such a deep attraction to a man, one that left her body trembling and longing for more. He was strong and handsome, and her desire was stronger than she had ever known. Her hand lifted to his mouth, her finger outlining his lower lip. She surrendered. Accepting her acquiescence, his loins began to ache and yearn as grasping energy consumed him with one unstoppable purpose. The detonation unleashed a carnal urge forsaking sense and reason. His pupils were dilated, his eyes fixed and staring, his hands lunged at her suddenly, grasping at her breasts, forcing them together with ferocious intent, biting her nipples. An uneasy mix of pain and pleasure that she had not experienced before, her body and face contorted in a rapture of fearful expectation.

A deep surging need rose within her pulsating labia and through the very bowels of her, causing her back and neck to arc away from him, her head against the tiled wall, her face taking the full force of the falling water. She submitted to his overpowering body as he separated her legs with his knees, pushed across her sternum with one arm and pulled the back of her buttocks towards him with the other. She offered herself to him, exposing her hot plump opening, unfolding herself with anticipation and invitation. He touched the sweet spot with ease, his fingers tracing her receptive clitoris. He thrust his hard cock into her with a confidence and expertise she had never known. She gasped, accepting his lengthy shaft. His rhythm and momentum deepened with each plunge in and out, gripping her insides. She was enthralled, in ecstasy. A statue, unable to break away from the intensity of his commanding.

Both her hands splayed out behind her against the wall, trying in vain to keep her body steady. His groaning and gasps matched her own, with each pulling and pushing, becoming louder and faster with urgency. Both grunting through clenched teeth, he clasped her wet hair in his hand to shore up his position as he released the last of himself with one last forceful thrust into her throbbing vulva. Now spent and satisfied, he let her body go. There was no kiss. They stood staring at each other, eyes widened, startled. The pace of their hastened breaths slowing together. There were no words. He turned around and left the shower. Roisin gulped. 'My God, what have I done? What have I done?' She turned to face the wall, the water drenching over her. Her thinking becoming clearer. 'Get yourself together. Give him ten minutes, time to leave. No one will ever know.' Roisin always thought this would be how it would end with James, after their spontaneous arrangement for sex was enacted upon hastily, and without thought of consequences. A quick exit, running away with a delicious memory to savour.

19

CUT AND RUN

Roisin inelegantly got herself dressed, giving her wet hair little attention other than a quick run through with her fingers. The clumpy knots would have to wait. She needed to get out of the spa and into the fresh air. As soon as she opened the front door, she caught sight of the tall handsome stranger leaning back on the wall with his arms folded.

'Hi,' he said, cocking his head towards her, smiling. 'I couldn't just leave. Well, I thought about it, but I wanted to know your name and see what you looked like with your clothes on.' Roisin stuttered. She was shocked to see him waiting for her outside.

'I thought I would just cut and run … You know, move quickly on, catch the bus home,' she said, trying to appear carefree.

'You can move quickly on if you choose, but you will never know what comes next. That was a heck of a first meet. Just think what the second time will be like,' he said, running his fingers through his hair. Roisin stepped closer to him. She thought he looked even more gorgeous with the hazy glow of afternoon sun falling on his face and dressed in a taupe Lacoste polo shirt and cream shorts. She reached out her hand to shake his.

'My name is Roisin Quinn. And yours?' she smirked.

'My name is Ian Hayden, and I would like to take you home. Maybe we could arrange another rendezvous. My car is five minutes' walk from here.' Once again Roisin melted in his sexy voice and the delights it promised, completely detaching herself from any sense of personal risk.

He directed her to a metallic green Audi Ur-quattro and opened the passenger door. 'I call her the green goddess,' he said, indicating she should get in. Roisin glanced in the back seat, noticing a black briefcase lying there. She supposed he was a businessman, probably married, taking his opportunities where and when he could. She asked him to drop her off on the street next to where the homeless refuge was. He didn't need to know where she was living. 'See you, Roisin, outside the same place, Tuesday night at seven, I'll be there,' he said with a wink. The green goddess took off at speed. Roisin watched it disappear and hoped that would not be the last time she saw Ian Hayden.

She can still remember how she tossed and turned all night long, reliving the encounter, still feeling his hands and body in every part of her, his smell and his movements playing out with her every breath. Exactly as it was the first night she had sex with James, that amazing feeling of wanting more of him. And that feeling that the first time would be the last. To Roisin's surprise, Ian turned up on the evening they had arranged to meet. She waited outside the sauna, dressed in a figure-hugging black dress, her hair styled long, with flowing waves swaying below her shoulder blades. She saw him from a distance, his powerful stride carrying him towards her.

As their eyes met, their smiles broadened, telling of how pleased they were to see each other. They embraced and kissed and went on to have the most exhilarating evening together, followed by nothing more than a kiss and a promise that they would go away the following Saturday and spend a week together on a beach in Dorset. It was a hot summer and they spent much of the time on Studland Bay nudist beach. Roisin found she needed fewer clothes than she had packed.

They bonked relentlessly through the best of the Kama Sutra, day and night, in the sand dunes, in the sea, in between the sheets. They had sink sex, sex in the bath, up the walls, on the stairs and, on the last evening, on the rooftop garden as they drank pina coladas and watched the sun go down. By the end of the week, she was drunk on his delicious, rugged body and worldly mind. She did not want to leave his side. The thought of him wanting to leave her she found excruciating. She was in love. Then he told her he had a wife, and that they had only just separated. She finally admitted that she was not living with a perfect mum and dad, brother and sister in a perfect home as she had told him. She admitted she was living in a mad house, that she needed to leave, and that she wanted him to help her.

After visiting Nuneaton, where Ian lived, Roisin trawled the town centre one Saturday, walking into every shop and pub. To her surprise by the end of the day, she had secured two part-time jobs – at Fosters Menswear and at the 88

Rush nightclub. She found a room in a house of multiple occupancy and left her old life behind.

Roisin believed what she wanted to believe, that every word Ian said was true: his wife had cut and run, after asking for a divorce, her decision; he was free to do what he wanted, and he wanted Roisin. The only words she heard were that he wanted her. Ian didn't allow her to come to his house when there was a chance his wife might visit to collect her belongings, except for that one evening when he knew his wife was staying with her sister in Scotland. Roisin walked from room to room, noticing some of his wife's clothes and possessions crammed into boxes in the spare room.

The house was too pretty to be a bachelor pad. A woman's touch was apparent everywhere she looked: the withered flowers draping over the rim of the vase, the bright cushions and floral-print curtains, the cute collection of pig ornaments thoughtfully positioned as one happy family. She gave little thought to being in the home and the bedroom of another woman. There were no alarm bells ringing in her head. There was no hesitation in ripping off her clothes and defiling the rose-petal quilt cover with the smell and sweat of her sex.

Within a week, the house was up for sale. She only stayed there on the weekend, arriving late and leaving early, never leaving her toothbrush in the bathroom or her knickers on the floor. Ian would lean over the bar of the 88 Rush club, watching her all evening while he downed pint after pint. He said it turned him on to watch her serve all the guys. He would hear the comments they made when she reached up, stretching to get hold of the thin neck of a glass, or bent down to empty the slops bucket of the overflow lager back into the mild. There was always a hard marathon bonk when she eventually fell into bed, even when she said, 'No, please ... not now.'

He never heard those words, he never stopped when she was sore, he just took her when he wanted. Once, when she tried to physically stop him in the middle of a session, he shoved a bottle of Southern Comfort in her face, forcing her to drink it, and shouted at her, 'Now shut the fuck up.' Still, the fear of losing him was palpable. Even though his controlling at times was too much, she mostly enjoyed the intense pleasure, the desire and worship of him. The need for him to love her was a driving force. This, she thought, was real love, the kind only a man can give. Everything she wanted and expected from a man was destructive, and she could not see it. A beast of a man, a raging masculinity that must be unchallenged and served.

She was blind to the fact that he owned her and was stripping her of all self-worth. She was standing on the precipice of her demise. One thing, however, was clear in her mind: the desire to find a secure place to live. Roisin thinks of James, and which parts of him remind her of Ian. She accepts he is controlling, but he can be challenged; he is masterful, but in a more thoughtful way and it was his mind and reputation that attracted her before his body. She knows a misogynistic, unintelligent man like Ian, one who treated her like a commodity, could never satisfy the woman she has now become.

Through dogged hard work and tenacity, she went on to buy her first house, aged nineteen. The sense of achievement she felt was immense, and the feeling of personal security and safety was something she had been searching for her whole life. The estate agent nodded and smiled in all the right places during their conversation and ended with, 'I have a daughter your age and I dread to think of her being homeless and without her mother and myself to support her. I can help you. I have a two-up two-down terrace that is up for sale. I own the property and no work needs to be done. It's ready to move into.' Roisin sat with bated breath.

'Really?' she said, finding it difficult to contain her excitement.

'Yes, really. I can give you the keys now. It's the perfect property for you. I will organise the solicitor and the mortgage provider … and help make the sale go through smoothly. How about that, Miss Quinn?' Roisin remembers being speechless when Mr Lews handed her the keys to the property. It all seemed too good to be true. She turned the key and took in the smells of newly painted walls and freshly laid carpet. Everything was new. She couldn't believe her luck.

Roisin found out a year later that luck had nothing to do with it. The seemingly kind estate agent had taken the opportunity to sell her a house that belonged to him, and which he knew had severe subsidence along the whole length of the house on the fireside wall.

Trudie, her friend from Leicester, who now worked with Roisin at the 88 Rush nightclub, brought a double mattress and a small black-and-white television when she moved in. After returning from a night's work, the young barmaids cuddled together under a blanket, falling asleep at four in the morning, in the glow of dying flames as the fire petered out. As time went on, Roisin realised she could no longer pin her hopes on a future with Ian. He'd made it clear he was buying a house only for himself to live in. He had changed. He had picked up with old friends who were single and had started wearing a gold medallion around his neck.

He had long been making the most of his sex appeal, pushing the limits. He thought nothing of letting women salivate over him, grinding into him, hands all over his chest while he leant on the bar, knowing Roisin stood watching, angry and jealous. It turned him on to watch women fight over his body. Roisin remembers Trudie spending hours telling her that he was no good for her, that he had tried it on with her too. Roisin cried time and time again, until there were no more tears … It was her turn to cut and run. It was over.

She left a note for Ian, telling him not to call at her house again. When she returned home, there was nothing left of him to show he had been in her life, other than a large bouquet of red roses on the kitchen worktop with a card attached saying, 'I will always love you'. The only time he ever bought her flowers and said those words was the day he walked away.

Roisin remembers the anguish she went through after giving so much of herself to Ian, hoping for loyalty and love, and being left with nothing but heartache and anger. She also remembers that it took her years to break his hold over her and realise this was not love, and that she had been used. There was so much she had to learn, but at the time she didn't know how to change.

20

I WANT TO KNOW WHAT LOVE IS

The first draw of blood

Roisin is once again feeling stressed and having nightmares about losing her home, a recurring dream that has haunted her many times over the years: her home crumbling on top of her, crushing her bones, burying her until bricks and flesh became as one pile of dust. Her insecurities are now strangling her, fuelled by the fear of being alone after she leaves James. Roisin knows that feeling: after her relationship with Ian ended, she had to become streetwise and learn how to navigate through the filthy pond life and the choking, nicotine-filled nights that had become her reality.

Ian was still there at every corner. She would often see him among crowds at the club, leaning against a wall, or sitting on a chair, taking a long drag of his cigarette and blowing the smoke up in the air while this babe and that babe wrapped their bodies around his lap, always a trance of ecstasy plastered over his face. Roisin knows there is every chance she will see James quickly moving on with his life, with another woman on his arm, dressed up to the nines, enjoying the best of him. She will hear about his every move, through gossip, and she fears the pain of lost love will eat away at her heart, just as it did with Ian. The thought of starting again in her late fifties, after it took so long to find fulfilment and contentment, feels harrowing.

Weeks after the split, while at a different nightclub, Roisin bumped into Ian. He was by himself. He told her that when he had said he would always love her, he had meant it and he began kissing her shoulder. He said he was leaving to start a new life in Spain and wanted her to come with him. She was desperate to say no, but she still loved him and wanted to believe him. She walked to his new house, driven by need, but afraid of what she might find. She was disappointed to see his bedroom walls were completely covered in pictures from girlie mags and there was a female mannequin dressed in a red silky bra and thong, suspenders and stockings, next to his bedroom window.

'Wow, an all-out bachelor pad,' she thought. Ian took her to bed on dark blue silky-smooth sheets that indulged her every sensory zone. Their night together was passionate and promising. His words spoke of longing, need and regret, against the backdrop of an album by Foreigner, climaxing in tune with the hit song, 'I Want To Know What Love Is'. This time she was sure this could only be love.

But in the cold light of day, as she lay alone on his bed listening to him making coffee, she realised that the night before had been nasty and cheap. She noticed the streaks of mascara marking both pillowcases. She was one of many. It was a game, his sport, and it meant nothing. He left for work without mentioning the words 'Spain' or 'love'. The last blow from Ian left her feeling cold, stupid and worthless. Soon afterwards, Trudie moved in with her boyfriend and a week later the bailiffs walked out of Roisin's house with her TV, radio and record player for being two months behind on the council tax. She felt crushed.

Roisin remembers a dark cloud coming over her that night. She was sitting in the only comfortable room in the house, drawn to the heat and glow radiating from the Parkray back boiler. Staring through the window out into the blackness, she felt loneliness and loss hitting her like a freight train. She felt dead inside. Roisin sensed those dark and desperate feelings once again overwhelming her. It was a time and place she had hoped she would never find herself having to face again.

Ahead, she saw only a narrow, broken window, a grey smoky light and sharp cutting edges to slash her life away. She pushed a knife into her left wrist, at a place she thought soft and tender, wondering how hard, and how deep she would need to push to reach a stream of red that would take her to a place of calm. She dropped the blade at the first sign of blood on her pale skin. It was the one time in her life when Roisin felt so desperate that she was ready to die. She curled up by the fire, falling asleep, losing herself in the twirling flames. She thought she was dreaming when she heard a distant voice. It was Darra. She cried with relief and threw her arms around him, knowing his timely visit had saved her.

21

LOVE REALLY HURTS WITHOUT YOU

One image that is imprinted on Roisin's mind and heart is that of Darra standing on his drive, unable to wave her goodbye due to holding a grandchild on each hip. His beaming face said it all, and Roisin was delighted for him. She had spent the day celebrating her brother's birthday at his home. On the drive home, she felt a twang of loss for herself and her child, and maybe a grandchild that might have been, but it soon passed. At the time, her cup was full. She had no inkling that one day her marriage would be in jeopardy, and she would lose her stepson. Roisin had felt such pride when she watched Darra marry Katy at the perfect wedding, and then go on to have two daughters, Maree and Lucy, and a son, Jonny. Even though Roisin is only a year older than her brother, she has always taken her role as big sister seriously. She likes who her brother is, she knows the bones of him, the anger rising, the self-destruct button and the reasons why.

He is damaged by the absence of a mother and a loving father, just as she is. Roisin believes her brother marrying young was his way to save himself from a life of drugs and crime. She knows he is a sensitive man who prefers to lock away the darkness of the past, for fear of it raging in his present. She watched him immerse himself in family life, passionately loving his three children and seven grandchildren. Occasionally she has seen the aftermath of his drinking too much raise its ugly head, threatening his peace and purpose, and would do her best to help him lock down the monster and the nightmares colliding within him.

When Roisin speaks of her brother, she refers to him as tall and ruggedly handsome, a doer and a talker who works hard and plays hard, a man who belly laughs and tries to sing like Tom Jones at parties. She knows her brother would never be impressed by a braggart with money and flash cars or a devious mind; his waters run deeper than that. His past, she feels, instilled in him the intuition to recognise who he should shun. On reflection, she also thinks he made better choices than she did.

Darra is never far from her thoughts, so when his wife Katy called Roisin with an urgent cry for help, she jumped to be at his side. It was during the early part of the pandemic at a time when they could meet face to face in the Halfway House pub. Roisin was shocked at the sight of her brother when he walked through the door. His hair was a thick mass of unwashed curls reaching almost down to his shoulders. His square chin was covered in a salt-and-pepper, roughly cut beard, and his front tooth was missing.

His eyes, despite expressing a deep joy at the sight of Roisin, looked red and heavy. He was still her Darra though, and she could still see his unmistakably handsome face and roguish smile beneath the rough. While grabbing hold of his jacket and pulling him towards her for a much-needed hug, she asked him how the other guy had managed to knock out his front tooth. 'He should have banged the gold one out while he was at it. Made it worth his while,' Darra replied, smirking. They laughed and held each other, pausing a moment with a shared gaze that only comes with the deepest trust. With nearly a full pint of beer in his belly, he finally let out a deep sigh. 'You know how it is, sis. I've been thinking about him a lot lately. Can't seem to get him out of my head. I was so wrong, all these fucking years, telling you to keep schtum, shut the fuck up and be grateful for what you've got. I'm sorry. He was a bastard, a fucking coward.' Roisin had always expected this day would come, the day when Darra would look back at the past and see what she saw, and feel what she felt about their father leaving them black and blue and at the mercy of his sick girlfriend spouting her vile abuse, and exacting the punishment she found the most pleasure in.

Roisin remembers that Darra, as a child, always internalised his pain. He toed the line until he no longer could, he ran, he hid, he stood up in front of her and took the blows, and he survived to walk away and bury the whole shitty experience. Throughout the years, Roisin has witnessed Darra strive for a life full of love, freedom and laughter, one with few restrictions and rules. She knows the pain he is now feeling is real, and all the deadlier now for revealing itself among those he loves. Something, or someone, every now and then, rankles the sleeping black dog, the darkness overshadows, and he loses sight of the way forward. He has sworn many times never to allow the ugliness of his past to disrupt the contentment within his family, but there have been a few slip-ups. Armed with her big-sister clout, Roisin would steer him through the mire, ensuring he stayed where he wanted to be, at the centre of his family.

Roisin lifted her brother's chin, so she could look him in the eye. 'I'm a monster, just like that bastard was,' he sobbed. Roisin listened as he told her he had battered a young man at work for humiliating him in front of the gang on the building site. The guy had hit a raw nerve by making a crass joke about Darra's dad being a paedophile, and that was it, he saw red. She could see that Darra hated himself right now, knowing he had put the young man in hospital with a fractured jaw and ripped lip.

'You're right, Darra, he was a bastard,' Roisin responded, with a reassuring squeeze on the back of his neck. Roisin knew Darra had never hit out before; this was about something else.

'I was fucking eleven years old. What dad lets their eleven-year-old disappear for six weeks and doesn't even try and look for them?' She recalled the time he was referring to, when he was crying and trying to tell her where he had been for six weeks in the school summer holiday. Their father had told her that he had gone with his friend Jack Collins to Glasgow to stay at his mother's house for a holiday. She couldn't understand why he had not said goodbye. She remembered how her anxiety had increased day by day, not knowing if Darra was safe. Her father had told her to stop asking where Darra was – 'not another fucking word'. His answers to her questions just made her think the worst.

Then one day, out of the blue, Darra had turned up, flanked by two policemen. They had found Darra and Jack sleeping rough with homeless people under a bridge. They were starving and ill from the cold.

Roisin clasped Darra by his cheeks and kissed him on his forehead, ordering him to get back to his beautiful life and go see that young man in hospital and beg for forgiveness. To do whatever it takes to put this shit back in the ground with the bastard, where it belongs.

After three hours of tears, and more drink than they should have had, Roisin and Darra worked through the anger together. She thought to herself that it only took him reaching the age of fifty-five, a pandemic, and maybe being told by Orla at Christmas that their mother was dying of cancer, to bring down the iron-clad wall, and reveal his long-suppressed feelings. Darra, looking even worse than when he had walked in, gulped down a last sob. 'Thank you, sis.'

Roisin watched him get into his van, and bellowed at him like a rowdy tart, 'And for fuck's sake, don't crash on the way home!' As she drove home, the whole scene played out again in her mind. To the folks sitting around in the bar, witnessing the dredging of emotions and the desperate looks and touches, they must have looked like a pair of forbidden lovers spilling out their last goodbye.

Roisin can remember many times when Darra has come to her rescue. At one such time, a single small gesture filled her heart with an overwhelming feeling of love and hope. She had been feeling utterly lonely, emotionally numb and tired from working long hours in two jobs, while also trying to fix up her house and garden with very little knowledge and a broken heart. It was midnight, the dance floor was hopping and heaving with high-spirited revellers. Roisin was desperate for the shift to end; she had a banging headache from the constant booming beat of dance music boring into her brain. Her hands were full of empty glasses that she had just collected from the corners of the nightclub, when she caught sight of Darra and Orla making their way through the crowds.

Her heart jumped. The sight of her brother and sister was the only drug she needed. She abruptly ditched the glasses and rushed through the crowds to greet them. They hugged and shared the biggest smiles. Before they released their embrace, the song that hit her ears was 'Love Really Hurts Without You'. They danced and sang together, soaking in the words that meant so much. The manager spotted Roisin's absence from behind the bar and summoned her to work. She did not care. The night was good, and she now had hope, because what she needed was finally within her reach. Darra and Orla stayed the weekend. When she needed her brother and sister, they were there to lift her up.

22

A TROUBLESOME JOURNEY

Roisin reflects on how she behaved throughout her early years, her choices in men, and why she was drawn to physical strength and arrogance, the type of man who had nothing to offer. She finds it difficult now to understand why she took such terrible risks at a young age. She wonders what she was thinking, having sex with a man she had just met in a sauna. She realises she could have been killed, could have been a statistic on the national news. It is only now when it is her husband who has enjoyed sex with another and her marriage is at risk, that she is able to see clearly and begin to feel a little of what Ian's wife endured. She never gave her much thought until now. She never met her and the only image she has of her is the one provided by Ian and by the photos that she left behind.

His wife, too, was no doubt the victim of his philandering, his controlling and dominant nature, and Roisin knows that she played her part in it. Roisin feels she deserved the following years of distress and longing for Ian, the ache of loneliness and the lying down, ceding to his wants. She let the vile beast tear at her jealous flesh relentlessly, diminishing and disabling her, taking her body and mind whenever and wherever he pleased, lying pathetically, grateful for his sweat. She was a fool.

For her twenty-first birthday, Roisin decided she wanted a fancy-dress party. Geeky Dave, her recently acquired eighteen-year-old lodger wanted to be her DJ. The party did not go as she had expected. Her house got wrecked by gate crashers and drunks who descended after kicking-out time from the Cherry Tree pub across the road, where she now worked as a barmaid. Darra got laid by the wife of a local ruffian, an older gypsy gal who told him to keep his trap shut or he'd be history. When she had finished with him, she pulled his pants up and said, 'Thank ye, boy.' Darra was scared to death for weeks, staying away from Nuneaton and checking his tackle daily for cauliflowers and shit.

Orla was raped, she thought, by some guy she did not know who left early, and later, sexually harassed by a geezer called George in a karate suit. Roisin was horrified to find her sister hiding under the quilt in her bedroom, sobbing, and George, the randy git, on all fours on her bed ready to pounce on her. Gloria, George's wife, a hefty type, grabbed him by the neck of his karate suit, pulled him off the bed, dragged him down the landing and shoved his head into the toilet, banging his head on the rim of the bowl a few times while shouting, 'You dirty fucker. You'll try and put your cock anywhere, ye fucking shite, you!' George threw up a few times while she smacked him about the head.

Roisin saw her chance to scoop up Orla, and the two of them escaped downstairs and sat in the kitchen. Roisin stood protectively in front of Orla, and ranted ferociously at the revellers for destroying her house with their cigarette burns on the carpets and beer stains on the walls. But once everyone had a cuppa and a bacon butty, they were all formally introduced in a rather cordial fashion and common sense prevailed. Seeing that the needle was still on the record as it turned round and round without a sound, Roisin was reminded that she had not seen Dave for a while. She walked into his bedroom and was shocked to see him looking green and deathly. There was an empty bottle of tablets lying on the floor. He had attempted suicide.

In a mad panic, she called the emergency services, and he was rushed to hospital where he had his stomach pumped. Dave later told her he'd got upset when he saw her snogging the bouncer from the Cherry Tree. He said he had a crush on her, and knew she would never have been interested in him in that way. Her house-owning dream was turning into a nightmare. The disasters came like the ten plagues of Egypt, torturing her until she had no option but to give up and sell up. First came the storm, ripping a load of tiles off the roof, then came the moles destroying her newly laid lawn. Then it got even more biblical.

She was sitting on the settee next to a friend with the amber of a thriving fire glowing in their faces. They were sat in silence, eating dinner from trays on their laps as they watched television, when suddenly a loud rumbling noise started to rise quickly into a loud and vibrating roar. In a split second, their eyes flicked towards each other and back again towards the fire, just as they were hit by a wall of black soot, which completely covered them and most of the room. They still had their knives and forks in their hands ready to pick up the next mouthful. They had no time to process what was happening, they were in shock and sat like statues for a while.

A man knocked on her door and told Roisin he had seen flames coming out the top of her chimney, and then it just collapsed in on itself. 'Better call the fire brigade,' he said, then left her to it. Roisin was in such shock there were no tears. She was glad of the fireman and his advice on her next steps.

And then came the flood, again biblical, but down to her actions rather than an act of divine intervention. The immersion heater had packed up, the thermostat was broken, and monies were low. Roisin decided to draw a sketch of the thermostat wiring and what screw went to what, and fixed it herself. It worked and she was so proud of what she had achieved. 'Who needs a bloody man?' she thought to herself, jumping into a hot bath in preparation for a hot date, which turned into a hot weekend away. When she returned home late on Sunday night, on opening the front door she immediately felt the room was cold and she could hear dripping water. The light switch did not work, and the carpet was squashy with water. 'Oh God,' she thought, as she felt her way round in the dark, searching for the cupboard where she kept the candles.

As she went up the stairs, the water flooded down over her feet. She didn't know where to turn next. There was no one to help her. Leaning against a wall, she cried her heart out. 'This fucking house! I hate it!' she screamed. She was resigned to the fact that she had no choice. She ran to the telephone box and rang her father and begged for a hundred pounds to pay an electrician. She'd had to turn to him when she was in trouble, something she'd swore to herself that she would never do. He cursed and grumbled and made Darra take the full amount out of his wage packet to reimburse him, leaving Darra with nothing.

The final plague that made her first house the house of horrors came in the form of rising damp that appeared on either side of the Parkray boiler. Over three years, the wall got wetter, and eventually the plaster fell off. The kindly estate agent, whom she'd thought had done her a big favour was a snake. He'd got his builder to make good the wall, covering it with a membrane that hid the fact that there was subsidence so he could get rid of the house. Roisin consulted a solicitor, who put a document under her nose that read 'for the buyer's discretion' as an answer to every question: it was clear the estate agent had screwed her over. She cut her losses, selling her first house, her house of horrors, for seventeen thousand pounds. She came away with six and a half thousand pounds profit, but would have come away with triple the amount without the subsidence.

The buyer put right the subsidence at a cost of fifteen hundred pounds and sold the house seven months later for thirty-nine thousand during the housing boom. Roisin was pissed as hell. With the luxury of hindsight, and not a worry in the world about bills and jobs that need doing around her beautiful home, Roisin can now see the funny side of her house of horrors, and thinks of the experience as character building. She is also aware, however, that James does not bother her with money matters, and it is he who keeps the ship afloat. Another price she will have to pay, she thinks, if she finds herself buying her own property again.

For Roisin, the years after Ian were as dramatic as an opera. They were marred by torturous religious guilt, and crippling loneliness. There was always a girlfriend or two who she would go out with once a week, careering around looking for the one true love, but money was so tight, and she was always the bystander, watching the fun stuff and progress in life happen to others.

Roisin wishes she had known then what she knows now: what a good man looks like, and where to look. But she knows that unless she is prepared to be alone, she will have to face the pitfalls of singledom in a modern technological age, where dating seems even more cutthroat. She may come to wish she was the kind of woman happy to spend her life without a man keeping her warm at night. She now understands that she always noticed the mysterious silent type, naively assuming there would be depth and layers. She wanted to avoid the men of a shallow and flippant nature, but she got it so wrong, always falling for the charm, the darkness and the drama. Roisin was her own worst enemy; she can see that now.

The winter nights were cruel. She felt helpless and forgotten. She longed for warm summer days and walks in the park where everyone smiled and looked happier. She rarely saw Darra and Orla, and this only added to her sadness. In her twenties finding a husband, or having children, was never a motive. She had neither the emotional nor practical sense to understand or covet the normality of family life or bringing up a child. All she craved was a little piece of something real, something special to her, someone to love and love her in return. She decided after she finished working in nightclubs and pubs, that Nuneaton was not the right place to find a good man. It lived up to its reputation after being voted the most promiscuous place in the mid-eighties, not just in the Midlands or in the United Kingdom, but in the whole of Europe.

Roisin got herself a chocolate Labrador and called him Fudge. Her new companion brought her a different kind of love, unconditional and beautiful, and she made a conscious decision to be celibate, and it lasted for three years. She was tired of having to explain why she did not want a man who was pursuing her, and she was not good at losing a man when she had just wanted sex. She did think one last blowout would be in order though, to give her something to think about during the sexual drought ahead of her. And she's never forgotten her one last blowout: he turned out to be the bonk of all bonks.

It was Saturday night. Her friend was 'bored out of her head' and was 'up for a hunting sesh', as she put it. The talent at the 88 Rush club looked desperately uninspiring; that is until the army boys walked in, wearing full uniform. Her friend went gaga and was lost for the night. Roisin cut through the squaddies and noticed the back of a green beret sitting on top of a thick-set neck and above a broad pair of muscular shoulders and a pair of arse cheeks to die for. 'Fuck!' she said to herself. 'Who are you?' Panting with intrigue, she decided it was now or never, and with her mission in mind, hoped that every man would indeed do his duty. She leaned back on the bar and with stealth-like manoeuvring sidled up to the unsuspecting soldier who was nursing his pint. She flicked back her red hair and angled her head towards him, throwing him an irresistible look.

He very slowly turned his head towards her and, keeping his cool, raised a corner of his lip, which was only just noticeable under his 'I'm in charge of the brigade' tash, and raised both eyebrows. 'Hello. Is there something you need?' he asked in a masterful gravelly voice. 'Perhaps a stiff drink?'

Roisin, feeling smug that she had got his full attention, replied, 'A stiff Southern Comfort will do for starters.'

'I don't dance or smooch, and I'm only here for one night. I'm taking the lads down to Larkhill Garrison in the morning. They're here for one last night of freedom,' he said, setting out his stall.

'You sound like just what I'm looking for,' she said, touching her top lip with her finger and then placing it on his. They wasted no time back at her place. He ripped his uniform off and ripped her dress off with all the gallantry and speed of the PT instructor he was. Dressed only in a condom, he executed her mission with the power and expertise of a nuclear submarine, and with the hardest guns she had ever wrapped her hands around, and the drive and duration that left her without a fight in the field. She was long defeated, and he continued to wrestle for more. Before sunrise, she opened her eyes to the touch of a tender kiss on her lips and his warm breath in her ear as he left her with his softly spoken words. 'It's a good job I'm leaving … You could give me a whole lot of trouble, you beautiful girl.'

She expected no more and fell straight back to sleep. It took weeks before the smile on her face began to fade.

The next time her friend had an Ann Summers party, she bought something to remind her of her long night with the rock-hard soldier and to keep her satisfied whenever she needed over the lonely years ahead. Roisin finds she can still get excited by the memory of him. She cannot remember his name, only that feeling of sexual enthralment with a hunky stranger. He was her fantasy, one only a single or brazen woman can live out without consequences. Now she knows James has been unfaithful, she is not sure she can stop her fantasies from becoming her reality.

After taking control of her personal life, Roisin began to focus her time on pursuits that used to matter to her more, like studying and learning new skills. She attended many educational and hobby evening classes, primarily to stave off loneliness and meet people. She tried her hand at quite a few different jobs in just a few years – fashion shops, factories, nightclubs and one particularly memorable stint at the family-owned Manor Hotel, where the owner taught her the professional way to scrub a loo until it shone. She had to make up fourteen beds every morning, return late in the afternoon to help the kitchen staff prepare dinner, and then stay behind the bar until after twelve o'clock, or until her husband decided to send his buddies home. She was waif thin, totally knackered, with zero social or personal time and the wage barely covered her bills.

The best money she earnt was at her next job at a shower company, but it was the worst for misogynistic abuse and humiliation. As her birthday approached, she knew her turn would come. Sure enough, a group of men dragged her out into the loading bay, watched by a lecherous management. One man pulled down her knickers and lifted her skirt, while another hosed her down with freezing cold water. The birthday ritual was only performed on the girls the management wanted to see half-naked and screaming.

Roisin fought like hell to get away but found herself pinned against a brick wall by men she had thought respected her. When the call came, their tribal coercions took over, and the blue coats and the white coats all revelled in their sick domination. She ran out of the factory crying and took the next week off. Roisin remembers how scared and sick she felt each morning as her clocking-in card clunked into the machine. The women could be rough too. Some were ruthless and uninterested in the girl with the big ideas who did not share their colloquial language or their small-town mentality; the girl who preferred to stand her ground alone, rather than yield to the baying pack.

It's a long time ago, but Roisin will never forget one of the most longed-for and glorious days of her life. After working for fifteen years at the shower company, oppressed by privileged nepotism and mindless petty feuding by bored employees, Roisin had her opportunity to release her pent-up frustration and reveal to a new director of a takeover parent company the truth regarding quality cover-ups, mismanagement and physical abuse. She lanced the boils, cleaned her wounds and relished every moment as she was finally able to use her power to unseat the perpetrators from their lofty positions.

Roisin feels saddened today, knowing all those years were wasted, but she tried so hard to find a way out. Her priority was always to keep a roof over her head. It was only when she moved in with her boyfriend Andreas at the age of thirty-six, that she was able to hand in her notice. With her head held high she slammed the factory doors behind her and ran for her life.

The present, Sunday 3 p.m.

Roisin looks at all the photos related to the shower company, rips them up, venting her anger, and chucks the pieces on the pile on the floor, onto the pile intended for the bin. She catches sight of an image from a time she remembers with some affection. She giggles at the sight of herself and a girlfriend, Sally, wearing their special constable uniforms and recalls the day the photo was taken. It was her twenty-fifth birthday and they were jumping up and down, playfighting on a single bed in the dormitory at the Leek Wootton police training academy.

The course took place over three days and the first day was her birthday. She downed a lot of rum and coke that night and piled into the dorm at four in the morning. Her first indication of the next day was a boot in the backside from Sally, who told her in no uncertain terms to 'Get the fuck up! You're making me late and you can clear up your own sick.' Roisin remembers holding onto her stomach, wrenching her body off the floor, wiping the sick from her mouth and staggering into the lecture arena in full uniform, fifteen minutes late and with an unattractive shade of arsenic leaching from her pores.

Straight after the lecture, she took part in an assault course, which was videotaped and later presented to the group. She was picked out as an example of how an officer of Her Majesty's constabulary should not behave. Though it was all very much done in jest, considering the course leaders were the ones dishing out the alcohol. Roisin had a vision of one day joining the regular force, but she did not fare well with the macho culture. It was a far cry from helping old ladies cross the road, and being trapped through the night in a riot van with five bored proper policemen was a bit of a challenge. When she became aware that she was becoming the focus of their entertainment, she bailed out and decided her labrador Fudge was all she needed to fill her spare time instead.

Roisin continues to pick through the photos, the poems and the letters, placing them in small piles relating to place, time and face. The jigsaw of her life begins to piece together in front of her and in her mind. She slowly skips through the years that have been, and the here and now, trying to come to terms with her journey and that of her siblings; the choices she has made and the losses she has learnt to accept.

Roisin knows she needs to be alone with her questions, as only she can find the answers. 'Where was my head at? … and what of my morals? Can I just forgive my actions and blame them on the absence of my mother and the anger of my father? Was I so naive and lacking self-worth, and more importantly, have I changed? And what of James?'

She wonders if he has been unfaithful many times before, and if he is just another older man she has pandered to. She questions whether the truth is now emerging: that there really is no equality in their relationship, and it is too late for change.

She muses on what might have been if she had noticed a kind and soft-natured man, one who could have become her soulmate. If she could have been their first and only love, the first and only one to be their bride and the one to bear their children, if only she'd given herself that chance. She knows the blame for her failures lies firmly with herself. She feels nothing now, only sadness at her willingness to give so much of herself and expect so little in return. And if she stays with James, she knows she has learnt nothing.

23

WHERE LOYALTIES LIE

The present, Sunday, 4 p.m.

Her mobile phone has been pinging all day, and she has been ignoring it. Three calls from Orla, text and voice messages left by friends and five missed calls from James. She knows she must call Orla, as she'll be fretting. They have always worried about each other and been one another's fail-safe. Roisin feels that no matter their differences, there is nothing like someone who understands where you came from, the nuts and bolts of you and the journey you have taken. With Orla, there's no need for explaining or justifying the moments of moodiness or discontentment. Orla has always said that her life may have been less eventful than Roisin's, but she has always been there, watching from the sidelines, and she remembers everything.

Roisin looks at the texts that James has recently sent. He says how much fun he is having with his friends, but how much he is looking forward to coming home to her. He tells her he loves her and misses her … His words leave a bad taste in the back of her throat now that she knows how disloyal he has been. She is usually at his beck and call, so she thinks he must feel that something's brewing at home. Either that or he didn't go cycling at all. She wonders whether it's all a front and he has taken one of his Russian hookers away with him. All boys together, covering each other's backs. She feels her anger rising, her thoughts running amok. This club and that club … all a charade, all cloak and dagger, hiding their infidelities and their real personas. She turns on Netflix and starts scrolling for a series to fill her evening. She decides that he doesn't deserve an answer telling him all is right back at home.

Just before Roisin reaches the crescendo of her emotions, Amélie calls her on her mobile, sobbing uncontrollably. Roisin takes a deep breath. She'd known this moment would come. She has known about Leo and Vivi for some time now. Vivi had bragged about Leo's urgent need to jump her bones as often as she would let him only three weeks ago, but Roisin wished Vivi hadn't told her. Now she is having to deal with her own betrayal. She knows how painful it all feels, how serious the consequences are. She did not want to be caught in the middle of two friends or be the one to reveal this dreadful secret to Amélie. Deep down, Roisin hoped it would become someone else's problem. 'It's Vivi. I know it's Vivi,' Amélie sniffles back her tears for a moment. 'They are her knickers. How could she do this to me?' she agonises despairingly. 'Vivi is having an affair with my Leo.' Roisin knows her deafening silence speaks volumes.

Roisin knew it was only a matter of time before this got out, given that Leo's behaviour was bordering on stalker territory. Vivi is trying to cut him loose, preferring to romp with Lawrence the Lawyer, who is well versed in the art of lying, acting and knowing when to close his case. She wishes she knew if Amélie would prefer to know the truth or not. Roisin is conflicted, and finding it difficult to deal with the situation without becoming the snitch, the bitch and the downright interferer; she feels the net is closing in. Trying not to give anything away, Roisin lets out a long, insincere sigh. 'Oh dear,' she tuts. 'Ten o'clock Monday morning will be fine, Amélie. See you tomorrow.'

Roisin feels the need to call Kenise. She always knows what to do in a crisis. After calling her repeated times and her panicked messages get no reply, Roisin begins to feel backed in a corner, dreading the thought of having to face Amélie in the morning.

Roisin notices that Bernadette's Ladies WhatsApp group is on fire, as are her Facebook comments. 'Anyone know what the boys are up to? They're all very quiet,' is the general theme. Roisin knows that Bernadette will not tolerate any nonsense from her husband, Humphrey. The thought of him leering at a breasty girl bobbing over his pint and his wallet would send her into meltdown. She's a good Catholic girl and a cracking divorce solicitor; Humphrey's days would be numbered.

The present, Monday, 8 a.m.

Kenise calls round at eight o'clock on Monday morning sounding chipper. 'In need of a quick coffee, darling.'

'Thank God,' Roisin replies, now feeling able to release her pent-up anxiety.

She is so relieved, and very impressed that Kenise still had her wits about her at midnight, after a heavy celebratory session at the Rugby Club with her team, to listen to her frantic voicemail messages. Roisin feels very aware that one lie begets another lie, and doesn't want to lose a fucked-up friend, or be seen as the stubborn stain by all and sundry, scrubbed away down into the sewage.

Roisin has never been able to turn down Kenise; she will drop everything at a minute's notice if she needs her. She is her oldest friend and university buddy, who knows and understands her very DNA, her every motive and soiled indiscretion. She needs Kenise's pragmatic approach on the tip of her tongue ready for when Amélie knocks at her door, which she is soon horrified to see is in just over an hour. Roisin wraps her arms around Kenise, giving her a big hug – 'Great news about the wedding ... so you finally asked him?' 'Yeah ... thank God he said yes,' Kenise replies, grinning from ear to ear. She goes on to mention that Theodore had already told her that Leo had let slip among the guys that he was having the best sex he has ever had, and it was not with his wife. A few more drinks and he fell over himself to tell them it was with Vivi.

Roisin and Kenise agree that Leo is the one hanging himself, and that it was only ever a matter of time. They agree that neither of them should reveal that they already knew, as it will be much worse for Amélie as she would see their silence as another betrayal. With the dilemma of what to say to Amélie now dealt with and realising she must leave in a few moments, Kenise brings herself closer to Roisin. 'I bumped into Andreas in the Ham Hock, at least two weeks back,' Kenise stutters, grabbing Roisin's full attention. 'Andreas ... he ... he has terminal cancer,' she says, pausing for a response from Roisin. 'Not long left, by the sound of it, unlucky sod ... and his divorce only finalised two months ago. He said he's desperate to talk to you.'

This is a lot for Roisin to process. She hasn't spoken to Andreas in thirteen years, although there have been many fleeting moments when she has seen him from afar and wanted to walk over, talk to him and break the ice. Looking down at the floor, she shakes her head, struggling for a suitable reply. 'Call me if you want to talk things through,' Kenise says in her usual bolstering manner and familiar reassuring smile, and with one last bear-size hug, she rushes off to work at the sports clinic. A few moments later the ring of the intercom diverts Roisin away from nagging thoughts of Andreas.

The present, Monday, 11 a.m

Long after Amélie has left, Roisin is left feeling restless. She plays over and over in her head how their conversation went. She told her about James and how he has betrayed her, partly so that Amélie would feel less alone in her suffering. But Roisin was also aware that she was struggling to feel and show sympathy. She was not as interested in her friend's dilemma as she should have been. She felt shallow and disloyal, recalling how she had been amused, rather than angered, when Vivi had described how she ensnared and seduced Leo. She made excuses for herself, suggesting that her head is too full of her own story, or that maybe her loyalty is fickle and easily forgotten, but she fears the truth is likely more sinister. Roisin has always noticed her husband's attentive touch where Amélie is concerned, and her flirtations have not gone unnoticed. She thinks it may be jealousy that has disconnected her compassionate side.

24

THE WRITING'S ON THE WALL

Roisin lies next to Jax and Coco in their beds by the hearth, something she often does. It brings her great comfort, snuggling close to her big, beautiful beasties. Andreas Brandt is on her mind. She wonders how many photos of him she has kept, photos she had put away in the case and has not looked at for years. She thinks back to a particular moment in time when she was wrecked with emotional stress, after finding out he had taken his newly revealed girlfriend to America for two weeks – a trip he claimed was meant for 'time to think' … or so he said!

She recalls ripping out all the photos of the two of them together from the albums in an act of fury, throwing them on his bed and, after a moment standing still staring, launching herself into a mad frenzy, tearing them all apart. It had the desired effect; she felt liberated from her distressed state. She slept better that night than she had in the previous two months. Later that evening, she cleared away the carnage depicting the last fourteen years of her life with Andreas and threw it all unceremoniously in the outside bin. She opened her eyes the next morning and was surprised to find there were no tears to hold back and no sickness churning in her belly and bowels. She looked out of the window in the spare room, where she had been sleeping for the past two months and saw a new day, a different future.

She planned a 'Fuck You', girlie party at the house, with the couple next door as the star attraction. He had won the title of Mr Muscle UK two years previously and was the epitome of narcissism, swinging his schlong about every Saturday night at the strip club for hordes of screaming ladies. His wife, the other part in their swingers, free-for-all lifestyle, insisted Roisin be the one to oil up her husband in her own utility room, readying him for his steroid-fuelled, sexed-up *Phantom of the Opera* show. His slippery body, cock and balls made the surface of her kitchen island rather slimy as he dramatically displayed his wares. Roisin only just managed to keep her mouth from curling into a snigger when she later saw Andreas prepare his 'dinner for one' on the same worktop.

Andreas remained unaware of her destroying most of their personal photos or the break-up party, just as he believed she knew nothing about his so-called therapeutic trip. Roisin surveys the few images of Andreas she has managed to find in the pile of photos on her bed. She looks intently at the two of them holding hands, the shared warmth in their eyes as they smile at each other. She remembers their togetherness and how that once felt. She reflects on the years she spent with Andreas Brandt, and how much she had once loved him. At first, she thought they were the same: two lost and wounded souls, both scarred by childhood rejection, both tortured by lost loves and loneliness and both craving love and yet cautious of giving their all.

Andreas was far from an open book and protected his feelings, always afraid of failure and further rejection. She thought she could save him and in turn save herself. The night she first caught sight of him, propping up the bar at the Belfry nightclub, he looked like a model in a men's catalogue, smartly dressed in a dark suit and open-necked shirt, his fair to brown hair full and just overlapping the rim of his shirt collar. He had an air of quietness about him as he stood watching those around him getting drunk and raucous. She kept an eye out for him and always admired him from afar, curious about who he was. He always left the club early, leading Roisin to think he was married.

Then, one Saturday night, she turned up in a cute black-and-white polka-dot, just above-the-knee dress, with Orla by her side. Orla was now getting fed up with her big sister waiting for Don Juan to walk through the doors of the club, and then leaving her disappointed, so Roisin decided to take the plunge and stand so close to him that they rubbed shoulders. She got his attention, and by the end of the evening she had his phone number, and a date planned for Tuesday night, and knew that he was single. He turned up at her house looking like Knight Rider, in a black Supra sports car. She was twenty-nine, he was forty-five and had two marriages behind him, but he was the first man to give her butterflies since Ian, and that was ten years ago. Remarkably, Roisin had stuck to her vow of celibacy for three years and every part of her was glowing when in Andreas's company. She found herself awakening from her state of self-denial.

They dated twice a week for a month, and he never once tried to kiss her, not even a peck on the cheek when they said goodbye. She considered him to be respectful and she admired that. When the time came when she finally found herself pressed up against his naked body, she was lost in glorious rapture, her three years of pent-up frustration finally released. She worried about how she would look to him in the morning. She crept into the bathroom in the middle of the night and ruffled her hair into a sexy, fluffed-up look, brushed her teeth and freshened her body with a quick whore's wash, anticipating an early wake-up romp. She loved his body and wanted him to love hers.

He didn't bale out when she was diagnosed with the first stages of vocal cord cancer that resulted in surgery and a paralysed laryngeal nerve, leaving her voice fragile for over a year. It was a difficult time for them both and their relationship teetered on the edge for months as it slumped into silence, but he stayed the course, and she loved him for that. Andreas took her to Turkey, her first holiday abroad, then Arizona, France and Florida. They shared wonderful times together. Roisin recalls with amusement the sex games they played every Christmas and on their birthdays. Their relationship was fun, but for seven years it was just dating, and on his terms. He wanted nothing more, no commitment. He was her next serious relationship after Ian, and she knew things had to change. Roisin gave him an ultimatum, he needed to show her he loved her or she would end the relationship. Rather than face losing her, Andreas arranged a holiday and proposed to her two weeks later in a church high on a mountain in Sedona. After they got engaged, she rented out her house for a year and then put it up for sale. Aged thirty-six, she was living with a man for the first time in her life.

Roisin put her money into his property and thought it would go towards their future together. For the first time, she talked of having a child and he just smiled. One benefit to finally moving in with Andreas after so many years dating methodically, twice a week, and sometimes taking three holidays a year, for the first time in her life she had the freedom to further her education and follow her dreams. Only now was she able to walk the path she had so longed for all her adult life. She turned to look at Andreas asleep next to her and realised she had never once experienced this remarkable feeling of belonging and feeling safe. For the first time, she felt that someone loved her.

Andreas owned a building contractor's business, and money was never a worry, while Roisin loved her job working part time as an aromatherapist in a clinic. She found helping others to be the most rewarding way she had ever spent her time. Her confidence and self-belief finally blossomed, and she felt she could follow her vision of going to university. She began a full-time access course to higher education, and suddenly her life was full of inspiration and the challenges of learning, which she took in her stride, and which drove her with more gusto towards her goal. What's more, she met so many new friends, including Kenise.

The following year she was elated to be walking through the gates of Coventry University alongside Kenise, embarking on a BSc with honours in physiotherapy, and after three years of studying, she attained a degree-level education and a medical career: the acme being a ringside seat overseeing a triple bypass and stenotic aortic valve replacement. Andreas was there by her side with Orla when she graduated at the age of thirty-nine in the ruins of the great Coventry Cathedral, her proudest moment. Unfortunately, however, from that point, her gilded life began to fall apart.

Her relationship with Andreas was fragile, and she had not paid attention to how his drinking had taken over their lives. She now understood that he had always been an obsessive drinker, and that her trying to convince him to change was futile. She came to see that he was self-absorbed, and the drinking made him solemn, and unable to communicate. She struggled to cope with his rollercoaster moods, his lack of understanding and his stubborn iron will, never listening to her cries for change. His controlling behaviour, lack of interest in her needs and lies about his infertility ultimately resulted in Roisin having to find an escape route.

She had to come up with a plan. Since, she has often wondered if there was another way out, one she could not see at the time. But other than forfeiting her whole being and sense of worth, she truly believes she had no choice. Her emotions were rife, unmoored and no longer anchored to logic. The all-encompassing need to be a mother at thirty-nine was like the Shanghai Maglev, the fastest train on earth. It could not be controlled. Nothing else mattered. This desperation could not be averted. She was out of time, her hormones raging within her, demanding motherhood. Everywhere she looked, she noticed men with their children. Nothing is more alluring to a woman when she is desperate to be a mother than a man tenderly cradling a contented baby.

She needed that man, that father, that beautiful soul who for her had been forever elusive. After much imploring, Andreas took a sperm test, and found he was infertile. Grimacing at Roisin, he stood up and stamped his fist on the consultant's desk and bellowed, 'I am not bringing up another man's child.' He left the room. Roisin's heart sank. She had expected the results as an old friend of Andreas's had told her that Andreas started drinking because he knew he could never become a father. She had been hoping against all the odds that they would have a child; Andreas would love being a father, and he would help her save him and save who they were together.

But instead, he had blackened her heart with one wretched act. The very same caress from the very same hands that had once satiated her desires now drove her away. When she returned home, he threw the car keys at her and told her she was to leave with only the car. She looked at her situation and it was dire. She had given him most of the money from the sale of her own house, and it had been spent on his house, the car and numerous holidays. Everything was wrapped up in his name only and legally he could throw her out on the street.

She was devastated, crushed by her predicament, one she had naively agreed to, thinking an engagement ring meant he loved her enough to consider her needs. She had been so wrong, and she was trapped. Andreas told her that if she could bury wanting a child, she could stay. After all her struggles to keep a roof over her head, she was now going to be homeless again, without any means of starting again.

With the passing of her father, however, came the promise of inheritance money from his house. Roisin used this money to pay for fertility treatment and persuaded Andreas to move house and then both their names would be on the deeds as a percentage shared ownership. By doing this she had taken back the right to fight for the home she lived in, and she would then be able to leave with a deposit for a mortgage on her next house. It was a deception she took no pleasure in. For her it was survival, taking only what she had put in and giving herself the chance to become a mother.

She returned to the same consultant and arranged artificial insemination. After seven months of secrecy and deceit, against all the odds, she was pregnant. She knew the consequences of her plan, now having come to fruition, would infuriate Andreas and she would have to take whatever came her way. When she heard those words, 'Congratulations, Roisin. You are pregnant,' she finally knew what the wonder and the thrill was about. Those three words, 'you are pregnant', brought forth a feeling like no other she had ever experienced. It was a heart-stopping moment, her life's course and purpose changed in one short sentence. Something so longed for, yet so difficult to process. Her whole being buzzed with excitement, and the way and the circumstances in which she had conceived faded into insignificance. She now had a different future, and she was elated.

Roisin remembers the stress of living a double life, balancing her life on a tight rope, waiting for everything to fall apart. The mixed emotions of delight and fear flip-flopping in her every day and night was a heavy load to bear. She tried desperately to keep her pregnancy and her joy secret, knowing the consequences were terrifying. She thought the stress alone would end her pregnancy and so planned to delay telling Andreas until after the first three months. She was not trying to trap Andreas into fatherhood, she just feared the fall-out. She had no time to leave him and start again. This was her last chance.

At her three-month scan, the heartbeat was silent. She was alone to hear this news and walked out of the hospital in despair. She sat in her car for an hour and cried a river. Andreas was sitting in the kitchen with her phone bill in his hand when she arrived home. He reprimanded her for going slightly over her monthly limit. He noticed her eyes were red and swollen.

'And what's wrong with you? You look like someone has died,' he chuntered, looking away from her. Roisin ran into the bathroom, locked the door and stood staring at herself in the mirror.

'End this madness now ... end it now,' she repeated to herself.

She told him her baby had died. Andreas, as she had expected, hit the roof. A week later, a gripping pain took her to the floor and came and went in fierce and violent waves, ripping the dead from within her. She rolled around in agony while Andreas, beer in hand, continued to watch the football.

'Not my baby, not my responsibility,' he chanted. Roisin knew their relationship was long over before she got pregnant, and that she, too, was accountable for the pain she went through, but she had hoped for some humanity and understanding. There was none. He had nothing to give; he was never that man. She managed to scream down the phone to Orla, who called the ambulance as the miscarriage took over her body. The second 'baby product', as it was referred to later by a nurse, left her body in a second eruption of pain in a hospital bed. The nurse insinuated there may have been a second foetus. A thought that filled Roisin with more anguish.

It was a Saturday night, so Andreas dressed up as usual and went out with his apparently newly discovered girlfriend. Roisin prepared herself to leave a man who had never appreciated her, could not see her, or feel her loss. Roisin was fucked up: no baby, another heartbreak. But this time, it all felt so sinister. She was full of anger; angry with Andreas for having the best years of her life and taking away her chance to be a mother and angry with herself for yet again not having the confidence to put herself first, to see she was worth more, and for not recognising failure and not being brave enough to walk away sooner.

No longer looking for the sweetness in life, she returned to her old habits, her self-destructive streetwise behaviour, taking what she needed, with little thought of the consequence. Bonnet boy, as she later called him, a handsome young postman who caught her sobbing in the back garden, asked her for a date. She dressed up for him, listened to his niggles about his mother nagging him and agreed they should pull up in a dark country layby and fuck on the bonnet of his car. During the process of the not-so memorable and frankly rather clumsy fuck on the slippery and chilly surface of his VW, all she could think of was the square box glistening above her head and whether it was a camera. When the deed was done, she hugged him like his mother would and felt only slightly guilty for using his ass to confirm her newly single status. Even now, knowing that that was such a trashy thing to do, Roisin still feels the inclination to act recklessly after finding out what James has done to her.

Roisin watched Andreas leave the house at six-thirty on a wintery Saturday night, humming from the expensive aftershave she had bought him. Orla and her husband, Danny, turned up with a van. Kenise arrived with supervisory gusto, and they set about moving her every material possession to her new Victorian semi-detached. Her plan, fraught and gut-wrenching as it was, had come to fruition. She had taken back the reins of her life. That night nothing was taken that would bring him to her door. All she could do was salvage her broken heart and her spirit and make enough money to pay the mortgage on the house. She left with a clear conscience and tearful relief. At last, she felt that no one could take away from her the security of her new home.

Andreas obviously thought he had been shafted. Roisin, always one for reflection, recalled how, all those years ago, she had glanced through the mass of writhing, dancing bodies and colourful strobing lights at the Belfry nightclub, seeking out the tall, broad-shouldered man with the brooding gaze. She laughed at her own thoughts and her foolishness. Always looking for confidence and languor, she was still attracted to a man who reminded her of Ian Hayden. The one thing she learnt, after Andreas, was never to give her whole heart, trust and security to a man again, and to wait patiently for a kind soul and not an easy-on-the-eye, buff bruiser.

Andreas married his girlfriend eight months after Roisin left. Twelve years later, after their marriage failed and as Andreas watched Roisin's light grow brighter and her wealth become his envy, Roisin and Andreas would once again come face to face.

He was a broken and tearful man, telling of the last few traumatic years and the brutal verbal abuse he had endured. And, surprisingly, his deep and persisting love for her, which apparently had never left. His wife, having very capably and efficiently dispatched two previous husbands, was fine-tuned in the art of keeping the house and the money pot. Andreas lost the home he always thought he would die happily in, and most likely found comfort in a bottle to numb his pain. It had taken Roisin years to come to terms with the fact he'd had a right not to want a child or have one forced upon him. After the betrayal, all that was left was lies: his lies, her lies. No baby. A parent, a child – a vision for heaven only.

For both Roisin and Andreas, the writing was always on the wall. She now wonders if the same could be said of herself and James. She feels there is every possibility they, too, will end up going their separate ways. After a sleepless night, plumping her pillow, toing and froing, and staring at the ceiling, seeing nothing but Andreas's face, his memory refusing to fade into the dark, Roisin decides she needs to see him. The finality of his death is a burden she needs to control. It makes the hard edges of the past soft, and the sharp sword blunt. Something begins to churn inside of her, like an ugly tapeworm awakening in her bowels, giving her no option other than to give it her full attention before it is too late. She needs to right the wrongs. Roisin is expecting

James home late on Monday afternoon; she will arrange to see Andreas after he is home.

The present, Monday, midday

It's Monday, midday, and Roisin is trying to put aside her sixty-four-thousand-dollar question, 'to leave or not to leave James', for a single moment, so she can take in the wonderfully serene and uncomplicated view of Jax and Coco sparring and rolling over from side to side as they tumble together in the warm hazy sun. Taking in the summer's air, she meanders around the grounds of her house. The dogs, alerted to her presence, bound over to greet her. She feels their wet noses pressing in the palm of each hand as they walk slowly, syncing with her relaxed pace.

Only a few more hours left, she thinks, to enjoy the stillness, the calm and to engage with the grandeur and gravitas of her home. Roisin snuggles herself into the oval rattan swing chair by the pond, taking in the wavering tranquillity of the swimming koi, and the brook framing the garden. Her eyes follow the outline of the house she has come to love, a place she helped to bring into being from the paper to the ground, to the style and luxury that now emanates from its walls. Roisin is living her best millionaire's life; she has everything, except a peaceful heart, and she knows now that money alone does not equate to happiness. Since meeting James, Roisin felt confident in her ability to remain faithful to him. She had endured years waiting for a love that was real, lasting and unbreakable – a love that wouldn't waver over a fleeting whim or a heated argument. Her resolve was steadfast; she trusted her heart would neither ache nor long for anything that could threaten to destroy them.

Now, thirteen years into a monogamous relationship, she finds herself increasingly drawn to the hedonistic rush of new sex – the insatiable thirst for exploration and satisfaction. However, upon discovering her husband's sexual exploits, her once-unshakable resolve crumbles.

After mulling over her relationships with Ian and with Andreas, and how painful and tragic both endings were, Roisin begins to think about how she will leave James. James will be home in five hours and Ethan the following day. The thought of herself and James turning their backs on each other and exchanging cruel words distresses her. She thinks of Ethan, he has been through enough. She decides to call Orla. Now that her head is clearing, she needs to tell her why she has been distant, and that she will be telling James their marriage is over.

A text message pops up from Kenise: 'We are all concerned about Amélie, she is not picking up, how did her visit go this morning, call me.' Roisin knows a reply by text will not suffice. To avoid bringing down the mood at the wedding, she has decided to wait until after Kenise is married before telling her close friends about her decision regarding James. She calls Kenise, aware there's a good chance their conversation will last a long time. She listens to the story Kenise is eager to tell, about having a sore bruise on her arse, fat lip and throbbing finger, all inflicted by a marauding mob stamping on her. Roisin states the obvious, giggling to herself, 'Well, you mad cow, playing rugby at your age was never going to look pretty.' Roisin never was the type of physio to run on the pitch with a wet sponge, let alone get battered while her face slid into grass and mud.

Roisin begins to tell Kenise the salacious details Amélie had shared. 'Amélie found a red silky thong hidden in the bottom compartment of Leo's toolbox. She went looking for a spanner or something to turn off the stopcock. Straight away she recognised the ensemble, and knew it belonged to Vivi. They had shared a room together last year at Ragdale Hall. She needed a lot of tissues, bless her.' 'Oh my God,' replies Kenise, 'so she knows … but why is she so sure it belongs to Vivi?' 'She says Leo's been sneaking stealth-like into the basement at all hours of the day and night,' Roisin continues. 'The sounds she heard were the mucky bugger masturbating, not a noisy grunting while unstiffening a rusty jar, so to speak. Well, Kenise, at this point I had a job keeping it together. The image of Leo, of all people, knocking one out over Vivi's knickers was too much to bear. I had to seriously lock my jaw tight, for what felt like hours, for fear of bursting into fits of laughter. While Amélie was spilling her guts, honestly, I think I stopped blinking for at least five minutes.'

'Well, I am astounded at Leo – but not Vivi. We all love Vivi, but we all know better than to leave her alone with our man. She's just a nymph, a femme fatale. She'd play the Virgin Mary, if the need arose, literally,' Kenise says, laughing. 'Oh, yeah, she'd be whatever a man wanted her to be…' Roisin says, 'Leo didn't stand a chance.' 'I agree,' Kenise replies, '… so go on then what did she say?'

'Well, she needed a gin and tonic. I needed a gin and tonic, my jaw was killing me,' Roisin says, still trying not to laugh, as she carries on.

'Amélie said she had accepted Leo having the occasional moment to himself, quietly coughing out a bit of frustrated relief. She said it saved her a job, but she said this was different, he sounded like a wounded animal caught in a trap – well at this point in the conversation, I imagined Vivi dressed as a dominatrix, tightening a spiked metal ring attached to Leo's todger – and then I choked on a wedge of cucumber as I finished the last swig of gin. I had to bolt to the loo, flush, and then I waited five minutes, pretending to have had a sudden colon spasm.' 'Thank God I wasn't there with you Roisin … can you imagine? – I wouldn't have kept a straight face.' 'That's not the end of it,' Roisin continues, 'Amélie said she had no doubt that that disgusting strip of silk, soiled with her beloved husband's ejaculate, her Leo, for God's sake, belongs to Vivi. "Who else," she said.' 'And yeah, she's right,' says Kenise, 'who else can afford eight hundred pounds for a Kiki de Montparnasse thong? Only Vivi!'

'I wonder if Vivi is aware Amélie now knows,' Roisin says, 'her, Leo … and Amélie will be at your wedding.'

'Wow, that's worrying, I'm guessing you didn't say, "Yeah, we all knew, but not one of us had a clue what to do." And who of us would ever have thought their marriage could be rocked to the core? They seemed so solid, so perfect together. What hope is there for the rest of us?'

The two women were silent for a moment, Roisin thinking of her now-doomed marriage, and Kenise questioning the commitment of her soon-to-be vows.

25

THE SPINNING TOP STOPS

*There's no surer thing than one day
following the next ...*

February 2020

Roisin remembers how it started as a whisper, a hum in the crackles of communications crossing continents, nothing that hadn't come and gone before, nothing that she felt would bother her family or friends, or interrupt their comings and goings, or clog the cogwheels of the daily grind and privilege of the UK. It was all happening so very far away, in a world so disconnected from her own. Covid-19 was just the latest virus, one that was thought to have originated in China. It was the last two weeks in February 2020. Roisin was skiing in Kitzbühel, Austria with James, and their close friends, Arrabella and Barnaby.

On the day they left the United Kingdom it had seemed like business as usual. They spent a week on the slopes, wallowing in glühwein, goulash soup, Germknödel, and a large helping of blissful ignorance of the events going on back at home. It was only after arriving at the airport, when they were instructed to wear masks, that they began to feel a sense of unease. The following day, she watched a news broadcast depicting the horrors that were playing out in Lombardy, Italy, where the elderly residents were being abandoned by staff in their care homes and left alone to die. The realisation that this terrifying virus might soon be rampaging through James's care homes began to dawn. James soon moved to a war footing and from that point never left the front line.

On 23 March, Roisin and James listened to Boris Johnson, the prime minister, tell everyone they must stay at home. It was the start of the first national lockdown. Roisin called Darra, Orla and all her friends. It felt so surreal, like her call might be the last time she would speak to them. Roisin had left the NHS and her private work and was working within James's business. When the pandemic arrived, everything and everyone went into overdrive. Roisin remembers the fear among the staff was palpable, everyone fumbling in the dark, waiting for the science, waiting for answers, and waiting at the front door for personal protective equipment.

There had been many times during her career when Roisin had cared for the dying and faced the death of others, but this was different. It was catastrophic and overwhelming, and the vulnerable passing their last days alone was inhumane. She watched as hospitals sent the elderly from their wards back home to die, in an attempt to save the NHS. Each day brought more devastation, and Roisin and care staff were pushed beyond their limits, burnt out and fearful for their own lives. She feared for James too.

He needed to survive in order to be at the helm and do everything he could to save his residents.

And then came the silence ... The deathly quiet gripped the roads, towns and cities. She enjoyed the quiet from morning until night, day after day, as it gave way to the sweet sounds of nature, the singing birds and rustling trees. Putting aside the misery and suffering of others, and the stress and burden she witnessed upon her husband's shoulders, Roisin took comfort in the tranquillity of her home and the time she had to reflect. She knew she was one of the lucky ones, with a large garden to roam in and play in with her dogs, a fridge and freezer that were always full, and the freedom to read and paint.

The earth kept on turning like a spinning top, but its beating heart was in peril and nearly came to a stop. Just as it stopped for thousands upon thousands, it stopped for William Landry, James's ninety-eight-year-old father, whom Roisin loved dearly, and Kenise's elderly father, Omario. And it very nearly stopped for Roisin, as her beloved Darra lay intubated, helpless at the mercy of the virus and grappling with an ebbing thread of life, with only his inner strength and an exhausted care team to save him.

Holding an iPad between them, Roisin and Orla battled not to say the word goodbye as he spoke his last words before being anaesthetised. She could do nothing to reach him. His forced silence took away his voice and his choice. Like a newborn, dependent on the breast and its mother's life-giving care, Darra's life was maintained by a feeding tube, the oxygen that kept him breathing and his heart beating, and the detailed numbers that said he was still alive ... although he was silent as if already gone. Roisin remembered only too well the helplessness that comes from being in a state of silence.

At the age of twenty-nine she had a hoarse voice, an annoying persistent cough, which at the time she put down to plaster dust and using a heat gun to strip off forty years of layers of paint, which may have contained lead, on her doors and staircase. It turned out to be vocal cord carcinoma, and she needed surgery. The operation left her cancer-free, but aphonic for a year. Utterly frustrated and deeply saddened at being unable to communicate, her relationships suffered; she felt trapped with her own thoughts.

On the night Darra was in intensive care, Roisin was at her house locked in the arms of her sister, imagining the unimaginable. Sleep was nowhere to be found; she knew so many were dying. Her heart ached at the thought that this might be the end – their strong, passionate brother taken down by a microscopic virus.

By morning every outcome had been played out in her mind, but the one she feared the most would not leave her. His death would be a crushing blow, leaving a world where his mischievous smile and sharp wit would never be again, where his strong hands would never build or create. As the weeks turned into a month and the agony of Darra slipping away seemed inevitable, his wife received a call. Government guidelines had changed, and she could be by his bedside. There were positive signs that he might pull through. Those words turned into prayers, and Roisin begged for his life. Eight days later Darra left the hospital, a shadow of his former self.

He had to learn to talk and walk again. His body had wasted away, but his smile showed he was in the fight, and she knew his family would be his motivation. Roisin used her rehabilitation skills to help rebuild her brother, and over six months he hung on to her every word and slowly returned to a semblance of the man he was before. While sharing a pot of tea in between exercise sessions, Darra grabbed hold of his sister's hand. 'It's been tough, sis, our greatest battle. In my darkest moment, all I could think was, death smiles at us all. All a man can do is smile back.'

Before he could say another word, Roisin added, 'You smiled, and you sent him packing, Bro.' They hugged triumphantly until her tears burst forth with relief.

26

NO SAVIOUR FOR NOAH

The present, Monday, 4 p.m.

Roisin knows it won't be long now before James walks through the front door. The unsettling anticipation of waiting for him to return reminds her of how she felt, waiting for Noah to return home on the day he died. After the last lockdown was lifted, most people were celebrating and impatient to return to their normal lives and be with their loved ones. For Noah, it was a normal day. He did what he did every weekend, said very little, and stayed in his bedroom, only venturing to the kitchen for food. He had been like this for a few years, isolating himself, refusing to engage, comply or seek help. He was always transfixed by his computer, in a perpetual world of gaming day and night. He seemed to be one of a generation lost unto themselves, living through the typeset of others, rather than experiences of their own.

Noah had a sadness about him, one which no matter the effort from his father, mother, Roisin or his wider family, was unaccepting of professional support or change.

Covid had no impact on him. He liked the fact he didn't have to leave his bedroom and go to his place of work. He had always been an introverted child and did not share the attention-seeking exuberance of his older brother. Outside of gaming competitions, Ethan, too, had difficulty bringing his brother into the real world of normal conversation and interaction. Roisin felt that Noah's computer and phone were like heroin, surging through his every vein, and controlling every thought process. His headphones were positioned permanently and purposely on his head to shut out the sounds of the everyday world. There were moments when she wanted to smash his technology to pieces, but she knew it would distress and anger him, and the hardware would just be replaced.

Roisin saw how the divorce had damaged him. He had become a young man, with ambitions and dreams, but he did not have the emotional mindset to navigate his journey. He shut every door, ignored every avenue that opened before him and, with an unrelenting stubbornness, only listened to the battle in his own head. There were moments over the years when Noah had lifted his head above the parapet, and his father had managed to get through to him. Plans were put in place, strategies were agreed upon, there was a nod of agreement, and then there was nothing. Roisin kept on trying to turn the tide, but to no avail. Noah would drive himself to his place of work, he was always on time and a star at his computer-based job.

It was a normal late afternoon for Noah. He returned home and, after a few moments in his bedroom, he came over to Roisin, who was sitting at her desk reading emails.

'Would you like a Maccy D's?' he enquired with a cheeky smile.

'Ooh ... erm ... no thanks, Noah,' she replied. 'I've cooked us spag bol, if you're interested.'

'Nah,' he said. 'See you later,' were his parting words as he walked away from her. She heard the front door slam, feeling pleased he had engaged with her, rather than just leave the house. She thought to herself that he sounded chipper and hoped that he might be starting to turn a corner.

An hour went by very quickly. Then suddenly, Ethan came rushing down the stairs frantically shouting Noah's name. Immediately, Roisin knew it was going to be terrible. She watched James as he charged after Ethan, shouting at him, 'What has Noah done?'

She stood close to Ethan, listening to him, distressed and trying to catch his voice.

'Noah has left me a voicemail ... a long goodbye ... saying he has nothing to live for and he wants to die.' Ethan shoved his phone under his dad's nose. Roisin held her breath, waiting with horror, listening to Ethan sobbing.

As James continued to listen to his son's heartfelt words, Roisin watched his face become contorted with anguish. James, in disbelief, slowly repeated out loud the first few lines of what he had just read. With each sentence, Roisin's heart began to rip open. She stood with her arm around Ethan, attempting to comfort him, while her own composure fell apart. The rate of her breathing soared, and the sound of her heartbeat thundered inside of her. Time stood still as she waited for James to utter his words. In his voicemail, Noah told Ethan he had gone off somewhere quiet, so he could listen to the birds and fall asleep for good. The fear and the dread sunk in, when Ethan told his dad that the voicemail had been left two hours ago. Roisin watched her desperate husband call his son repeatedly. She got in her car, and drove, frantically searching for Noah's car.

The early evening dimly lit sky was like an abstract painting of blended oranges, yellows and soft red stripes. Roisin hurtled down country lanes, speeding around every bend, stopping at the gates of fields, the dark recesses in hedges and the narrow off-road tracks, surprising other drivers, and braking aggressively when faced with flashing headlights and beeping horns. She drove through the village to the nearest parks, anywhere she thought Noah might be parked up, where he could hear the goodnight birdsong before the darkness of night descended upon him. He was nowhere to be found. By the time Roisin, Gabriel and Freja, who had also been searching, had returned to the house, the police were sat talking to James and Ethan.

They had a search party underway, and a helicopter scouting the wider areas. Four hours later James got the call they had all dreaded. Roisin watched James drop his phone, lower his head into his folded arms, and wail like a wounded animal. Roisin wrapped her arms around him, shaking, unable to comprehend what had just happened, while Ethan, aghast at hearing his brother had taken his own life, stood with both hands over his mouth, frozen and staring into space. Noah had succeeded in his quest to die. And James, now lost unto himself, descended into a deep grief. Roisin and Ethan, grief-stricken, still waited, and watched for Noah to walk through the front door. The house, once a home, was bereft of light, and the darkness encircled them all.

Every minute of every hour, every possibility and every lost chance was regurgitated, taken apart and put back together again, searching for a way the outcome could have been different. 'What did we miss? How could we have stopped him? Was there someone else that he may have listened to?' Roisin could not hold father and son and herself together as one. Each had a different way of dealing with the tragedy. They drifted apart when they needed to pull together. It was only on the morning of the funeral that Ethan, flanked by his mother and father, began to release his emotions. They carried him through the day.

When Roisin came face to face with Talia, the two women embraced in their grief. Talia was inconsolable. Roisin felt overwhelmed with guilt. She had had a child, maybe not her child, but a child set to become an adult, with his whole life ahead of him. She had failed to save him and knew she would never be able to forgive herself. Looking deep into his mother's eyes was a dreadful and painful task. 'How can she forgive me?' Roisin asked herself. 'How can she forgive herself?'

Roisin sat next to James, holding his clasped hands tightly. He was unable to stand at the pulpit; he was broken. Reverend Paul spoke his words for him. Roisin looked up at the statue of Christ overlooking the congregation, his sad figure draped over the cross, a symbol of death and grief. She lifted her eyes up to the heavens and spoke silently to God, 'You saved your Noah, by helping him build an ark; your son, too, suffered, and you let him endure the pain of death, but you saved him too and brought him back to heaven … but for our Noah, there was no saviour.' For Roisin, the words of Norman Cousins – 'The greatest loss is what dies inside us while we live.' – later resonated in her mind and spoke to her of a lost life, one that never came to know the joy of how to live.

. . .

In her grief, and recalling his restless mind, Roisin wrote a poem about Noah.

A Restless Mind

The boy was lost unto himself, locked away in a restless mind
His view remained staid, snared in reluctance to change
Roaming the digital world, the spoken word, never able to find
Reality and kin, his preference to further estrange
Muzzled and deafened, always seeking a way to escape
His world, a fantasy, and a never-ending filename
From a child to a man, his needs become his heartache
No matter what the years, he lives each day in a video game
The time comes when his silence turns to grief
And what's missing, all but a stabbing pain
He sees no open door, no answers or succour of relief
Only a battleground before him, of this life, nothing left to gain
In a veil of blackness and a mind only for sleep
A long goodbye is all he can muster
And a memory short, for all those saddened to keep

Roisin, 2022

27

GIVE GROUND

Is it all about Noah, the crisis of their lives?

Roisin has reached the latter third of her life, a time when she wants for nothing. She has the wisdom to build and create stability rather than tear down and destroy. She possesses a freedom like never before. The choices are all hers to make. She has no money worries, she has status, and she is dearly loved, or so she thought.

Roisin has access to a world of opportunity. She knows only a blithering fool would wish for a moment of reckless wanton dirty pleasure. And James, she reasons, is that fool. For what is mere sex, if not moments here and there, a sharing of nakedness and a stroking of one's ego, something fleeting but something deadly if in the end it means nothing.

Roisin sees forbidden sex as the two sides of the coin, two faces with different outcomes. It's either cheap and nasty, and often can be overlooked, but then comes the question, 'Am I so worthless and disrespected, that he sees losing me as a worth the risk? Or, if it's a passion too hard to resist, and too real to let go, the deceit cuts much deeper, leaving festering wounds. But he's more likely to be seen as a good man who fell at the last hurdle, and whose torment was real: I was hard to give up. We were, and we are, worth something.' Roisin thinks for some women it's the difference between a long hatred and a long forgiveness; it depends on the woman, or the man, betrayed.

For Roisin, her respect lies in what her husband gives, and not what he selfishly takes away, even if it is a piece of his heart. The fact that he had sex with prostitutes does not bode well for the salvaging of her marriage.

It's six o'clock. James has texted that he has collected his luggage and will be home in thirty minutes. She charges upstairs to her bedroom, flings the case on her bed and begins to scoop up the photos in a mad frenzy. She picks up all those that have tumbled on the carpet and found their way into the crevices and folds of her bedcovers. She wants to avoid James walking into the room and firing questions.

She knows his prying will trigger her emotions and her line of defence will come crashing down. Fearful of what's to come, she questions whether the moment he walks through the door is the right time for a big showdown. But she also knows she cannot go on pretending they are OK. She needs to think quickly about what she is going to say and do; she grabs a gin and tonic.

She sits in her art room opposite her easel and the painting depicting her much younger self. She stares into her drink, looking through to the bottom of the glass, thinking about who they once were, what they have become, and the crisis of Noah. Was it all about him or was the diminishing of their love always going happen? She knows the thirteen years she has spent with James, seven of those as husband and wife, have been a gift. They have not been perfect, there have been challenges, but she has always wanted her husband and has always wanted to be his wife. It has been a rush, a whirlwind, but with time and an ageing body, she has longed for quiet, for serenity and a listening and attentive ear. James has been hell-bent on packing out every day. She has always known he does not do contemplating very well and sees little value in patience and languishing.

And with their differences comes a splitting of minds, a tug of war in which one party will always fall on their face. She has stopped waiting and longing for compliments. She knows he has stopped noticing her, and that his desire for her has waned. It is less obvious where she fits into his life and into his heart. She watched the cracks of her marriage begin to widen but felt powerless to change their direction. She knew she was becoming frail, her inner strength crumbling, weakening her reasoning and her resolve. She had come to see Noah as her son too, and losing him tipped them both into a very dark place, a place they had never been before, a place where thoughts were left unshared, and the silence became a wall.

Roisin, waiting in the wings, hoped the smog of tragedy would begin to clear, but it never did, and she now realises there is more to it than Noah and that the end of their relationship is imminent. The shivering fear of her new reality, of revealing to James that she knows of his betrayal, the escorts with whom he found solace. This will be their undoing. The sugary sweetness of life will melt away like candy floss. Her distracted husband and his abating love will leave her diminished and irretrievably broken. Her head rages with pain and she begins to retch out the sick in her stomach. Once again, she finds herself at the mercy of a man holding her emotions and security at ransom.

She remembers how her relationships with Ian and Andreas both ended, and how painful and dreadful it all was. She desperately wants to avoid a long and drawn-out suffering, in which she and James end up hating each other. She starts to think of an exit plan, one without schemes and deception, or malice to rupture their sanity. She receives a text from James; he has arrived home. Feeling stressed, she heads downstairs. Roisin lets out a deep sigh as she watches the electric gates part from the kitchen window.

She recognises the car pulling up on the drive. It belongs to Roland, his so-called financial friend, who was responsible for providing James with Russian escorts. She feels a knot in her stomach, and a heat rising into her neck, knowing the two of them together colluded in her humiliation. It is only the sight of Barnaby, her good friend Arrabella's husband, that stops her exiting the house at speed and confronting James and Roland. She looks at James and thinks he seems so happy saying his last goodbyes to his friends. He has more facial hair than when he left, which she always thinks makes him look more handsome.

She wonders if James will be her last hoorah, the last

man she takes to her bed and to her heart, her last real love. As the front door opens, she wonders one last time if they are worth saving.

'Phew! Am I glad to be home? I've missed you, Roisin,' James says, looking perplexed, as he rolls his suitcase over the hallway tiles. 'You never answered my calls,' he says, opening his arms to her, beckoning her towards him. 'Really? No welcome home hug?'

She has rehearsed the words that she might say in this moment a hundred times, to ensure clarity and composure. She has considered all the responses that he may direct towards her, the lies, the cover-ups, the insults, suggesting she is behaving like a neurotic woman, a woman with nothing better to do with her time than imagine far-fetched fantasies. But these words are not yet ready to roll off her tongue.

She walks into their bedroom and sees he has laid a clean shirt and a pair of trousers on the bed; he is taking a shower. Ethan is away until tomorrow, so she must say what needs to be said today. She knows James will want to catch up with work now that he is home, so she makes her way to his office and waits for him there. Moments later he walks straight past her. He is talking to someone on his phone and appears agitated.

'Just a minute, darling,' he says. 'It's Roland. He's not taking no for an answer. I told him on holiday I'm done with the London job. The profit forecasts are looking bleak. Anyway, are you talking to me now?' he asks in a sarcastic tone. She throws him a glare that grabs his full attention. 'What?' he asks, putting down his phone.

Roisin empties the contents of the envelope she is holding in her hand onto his desk. The printed screenshots of his messages and the images prove his infidelity. As she leaves his office, the only words from her lips are, 'I want a divorce.' James follows her into the spare bedroom and pleads with her to listen to him. He begins to tell her how sorry he is, and that he's been an idiot and never meant to hurt her. He tries to sit next to her on the bed and hold her hand. She pulls away from him. 'I've missed you ... I've missed us. It's Noah, but not just Noah ... It's me ... Nothing seemed to matter anymore.' He notices the suitcase by the bedroom door and looks back at Roisin. She takes in every bit of emotion he shows, every quivering word and fearful expression, but all she feels inside is an empty sadness.

She tells James her heart is breaking, and that he is not the man she thought he was. Outwardly she is calm and trying to avoid a fight with him. Her cold demeanour tells her what she feels, that he is no longer worth fighting for. She picks up the suitcase and tells him she is going to see Andreas.

'Have you been seeing Andreas?' James questions her, suddenly very angry.

'I haven't seen him since we met. He's dying. He's just another man who was in my life, and who I now need to say goodbye to.'

She tells James that she will stay with Arrabella for a few days and will then head to Kenise's wedding with her friends, and that she will let everyone know he will not be attending. And then she leaves the bedroom with her heart in shreds and an overwhelming sense of doom. It felt as if a knife was plunging into her guts, gouging out her insides, tearing at her flesh, ripping her life apart. 'So, this is what leaving James feels like,' she tells herself. 'I am broken.'

28

YOUR STORY IS MY STORY IS OUR STORY

After ignoring James's calls and beseeching messages, and spending a very tearful two days with Arrabella, Roisin is glad to be getting on a plane and listening to her friend's exuberance and frivolity. The last thing Roisin wants to do is go to a wedding and witness the sharing of love, loyalty and eternal promises. Her heart is breaking. Her own marriage is falling apart, and she is on course to lose everything. But she cannot let her own distress stop her from being part of her dear friend's special day. Roisin had encouraged Kenise to ask Theodore to marry her after their trip to Marbella as she feared her friend might lose him. She is so pleased that Kenise will now have the wedding she has dreamed of on the beach in Barbados.

Roisin fights hard to keep her emotions in check, keeping up the pretence that she is very much in control for the sake of appearances. She knows her friends Arrabella and Vivi will keep silent on the matter for the sake of Kenise, and she must do the same. Amid the surround sound of an excitable wedding party that is filling the plane, Roisin finds she is still able to close her eyes and drift into her own thoughts. Her heart, already laden with her own grief, is now heavy with thoughts of Andreas. It feels like a lifetime since their relationship ended, yet it is only two days since she sat by his bedside in the hospice as he passed away. He was a frail and tearful man. Roisin hung onto his every word as he told her, that over the years, she had been on his mind, he had regrets the way they had parted and he felt he should have tried to support her to have a child. He had, as Roisin expected, found comfort in a bottle to numb his pain.

Roisin relives the hours she spent by his bedside, holding his hand, taking in what little he could give. With all the drama of an operatic reckoning, the light of day faded as Andreas faded away. With a last caress and a loosening of their hands, their story was finally over. They had put aside the people they had become to each other, and she was glad she had been able to share with him on this, his last day, all the love and adoration which had flowed so easily when they first met. It was time for forgiveness and peace.

Surprisingly, the tears now streaming down her face go unnoticed. She dries her eyes with a blanket and stares out through the small window into the distance, way above the clouds, thinking of the finality of death. She imagines that it will be herself, or James in that same situation, watching the other from afar, loving someone else, filled with regrets, because neither of them has the courage to stand by the other.

Roisin walks with the bridal party through the powder-pink archways of the 1940s mansion with their suitcases. She gazes around at the great house, noticing its original colonial character, high ceilings, bay windows and plantation shutters. She sees that the wedding venue, set in Cobblers Cove, Barbados, is a haven of beauty and serenity. She manages a smile, as she watches her friends swoon over the beautiful naked statues that appear within the secluded gardens. As hard as she tries, Roisin fails to enjoy the pleasures of her surroundings. Her thoughts are elsewhere, thinking of her own loss, of losing James and her family. The ladies arrive at the private beachfront suites. Roisin takes in the warm and comforting sea air; she longs for solitude.

Vivi, being mischievous as always, threatens to leer at Leo, just for devilment. Roisin is not in the mood for listening to her treacherous marriage-wrecking behaviour, and her veil of pretence begins to slip, revealing her sadness. She cries off the evening's celebrations, claiming to have a headache and spends the night crying into her pillow, trying to avoid answering James's messages that plead with her to get in touch. She knows she has to attend the wedding ceremony the next day, no matter how she is feeling.

She lies awake at sunrise, desperately trying to put aside the turmoil she is feeling so that she can present herself as a joyful friend. With her makeup on and her best foot forward, she walks along the cobbled path leading to the enchanted and beautifully decorated tropical-flower pergola, whitewashed chairs and ivory silk canopy, where Kenise and Theodore will share with one another the promise of eternal love.

Roisin catches sight of Amélie and Leo. They are arm in arm and smiling at one another. She must have forgiven him, she imagines, or maybe he is on a tight leash and is working hard to gain his wife's forgiveness and a place back in her bed. She wonders for how long James will beg for forgiveness, or will he soon seize the opportunity to walk away from their marriage. She fears he will take the easy way out, putting his own feelings first and not fighting for her, just as Andreas did when she wanted to become a mother. And then, very quickly, finding a replacement to warm her side of the bed, just as all men seem to do. She thinks James, too, does not deserve her. He only had her to consider and love. She feels she has given her all to him and his family, and he has let her down … just like Ian and Andreas. She sees history repeating itself. For Roisin, the real value of life and love is genuine honesty, loyalty and love. And, as for money, it can sometimes tarnish what's real, and should never be at the heart of each breath taken, or behind each decision made.

The morning of the wedding is awash with glorious sunshine, the air filled with the scent of tropical blooms and the ocean. The guests are all seated. Suddenly the padre asks everyone to stand and greet the bride and groom. As the wedding vows are shared, Roisin feels a rush of emotion swell through her heart, not only joy for her friend, but also the memory of her own wedding day and the moment she and James, so much in love, spoke the same promises, with the same expectation of being forever in love as one.

She allows her tears to fall, and she soon realises they are tears of sadness for herself, and not tears of joy for the bride. She cannot bear the thought of what lies ahead when she returns home. She is so hurt and angry with James for running away from her, rather than supporting her; for finding comfort in the arms of another, rather than consoling her; for letting their lives fall apart, rather than being the glue that makes them stronger. But, above all else, she wishes that James would have let go, and allowed her to shoulder his unbearable grief, and carry him through the death of his son. She begins to think about what forgiveness would look like, and wonders if she will even have the chance to see if it's something she can do.

The girlfriends share one last drink together with Kenise before she retires to her now waiting husband.

'Here's to our friendship,' Polly proclaims, raising her glass. They clink their glasses and together they chant their motto.

'Your story is my story is our story. Here's to Kenise and a long and happy marriage.'

'Whatever happens with James, Roisin, I will always be here for you,' Kenise whispers in her ear.

'I know,' Roisin says, pulling her loyal friend close to her. The five of them entwine themselves together for a group hug. As Roisin, Arrabella, Polly and Vivi walk back to their suites, Roisin's thoughts are of James and how much she misses the deep love they once cherished. The tears rolling down her face don't go unnoticed. She feels Arrabella place her hand into hers, as she tells Roisin to come with her down to the beach.

They sit together on the sand, under a moonlit sky, listening together to the soothing sound of undulating waves. Roisin and Arrabella talk for hours of life and love, and how the vast ocean before them represents both.

Arrabella speaks of the tide rolling in and out every day, sometimes calm and safe to swim in, and other times choppy and wild. She talks of how you must wait out the storm, and of the times when a life jacket is needed, or you will go under and drown.

Arrabella turns to face Roisin, and she wraps her arms around her body, squeezing her tight.

'I am your life jacket, darling,' she says, 'and I'm here to stop you going under. And I can see James out there too, drowning. We have a second life jacket,' she tells Roisin, who by now knows the question that's coming.

'I would swim out there and save him too,' Roisin answers, her tears flowing, washing away her anger and resentment, allowing her heart to have its say. 'I have never stopped loving him.' She wipes away her tears.

'So, what are you waiting for? Get in that lifeboat, with James, and row your way back to safe shores.'

With Arrabella's last words firmly fixed in her mind, Roisin arranges a flight back home the next day.

29

THE FIRESIDE DOG

When Roisin arrives home, she finds James is not there. Home means everything to Roisin. It is the thing she has craved all her life, the formidable sense of safety and security when you own your own home, the strength of that feeling, the empowerment, contentment and, most importantly, the comforting sense of belonging it brings. She remembers the moment she stood with James in front of the old and broken gate to a rundown bungalow sat on a three-acre plot which became the land on which they built their home together. Building her own house was beyond her wildest dreams. The excitement and rush of creating an abode to her own taste with no set budget was a luxury she could never have imagined.

And there was always a dog lying next to the hearth, benefitting from the warmth of the fire's glow, or roaming the grounds, enjoying their domain. Roisin's majestic and much-loved Doberman, Jax, lies wrapped around her body. Her lips feel the softness of his ear, and his earthy smell fills her nostrils. Her hand moves slowly over his huge barrel chest, searching for his heartbeat. With a contented grumble, he lifts his head slightly and rubs his nose gently into her arm, his soulful eyes fixed on hers until he falls asleep. Coco lies on her opposite side, contentedly suckling a blanket. Roisin is lost in the moment; the overwhelming serenity and love she feels for her companions is priceless. She never wants this memory to ever leave her. She holds Jax and Coco close and wrestles with the thought she cannot now bear to see as inevitable: leaving her cherished home and her beloved dogs behind.

Roisin questions how many memories one can retain. They begin to blend and, with time, dilute and fade. The times she remembers are the times when the funniest thing, the scariest, or the most remarkable thing has happened. Her more recent experiences may have been grandeur and Michelin star, and the infinite decadence and self-gratification may now feel unexceptional, but it will always be her wedding day that was her most perfect day.

While occasionally she still feels at odds with her past and the implausibility of her present, Roisin tries to remind herself how well she seems to fit in among the highbrow circles. The ladies that lunch and the ladies that misbehave, and the men who have a club of every kind for every game they wish to play. She has felt the years roll by at a heady pace. And while she has an appreciation of wealth and indulgence, she also has a longing for a lazy day in a field of grass full of daisies and buttercups, looking up and searching the blue sky, taking in the sounds and the smells of mother nature, slowly, without interruption, without a plan or a thought for time. That, for her, is living, and she wonders if James will ever feel the same way.

Coco suddenly jumps up, alerting her to James's presence. He is looking down at her, his eyes glazed with tears. He drops to the floor beside her, taking hold of her hand.

'I don't want to lose you. I love you. This is our home. We belong together. Please forgive me. I know what I did was so wrong, and not who I am. I'm so sorry.' The wall that she had built around herself now feels less impenetrable. Roisin looks deep into her husband's eyes, as she searches for how to respond.

'Then tell me, James, how am I to kiss you, touch you, and know your mind is not elsewhere? How am I to trust you, thinking your body has been in the arms of another? What do I do with the grief, the heartache and the memory of what I saw on your phone?'

She finally breaks down, releasing some of her anguish. 'Love is not like the pages of a book, moving to the next chapter, always wishing for a happy ending to the story. You must trust your story, believe in your journey, know that the pages at the end of your story are not torn or missing. I no longer believe in our story, James.' She looks at James. He shakes his head. She waits, but he doesn't have an answer. She needs an answer. She is tired of carrying their love on her shoulders, and tired of waiting for him to step up and see and feel what she has known for a long time: that they are at their end. His silence speaks of his guilt, not his regret. He has cut the last thread tying her heart to his. No longer able to look at him expecting her to piece them back together, Roisin is brimming with anger. She leaves the house and goes for a very long walk in the park until the sun settles.

The freshness of the air, and the wonder around her, dries her tears and calms her mind. A mind that now seems sure she has nothing left to give. Her battle is over. On the way back towards the entrance gate, she catches sight of James walking towards her. He comes to a stop in front of her and lifts both of her hands, placing them in his. He tells her how much he loves her and feels dreadful for what he has done to her. He tells her he does not want their love story to end, he wants them to grow old together, he wants to always be by her side, looking after her, making more memories.

Roisin watches as tears began to roll down his face. She feels her hands moving within his, responding to his touch. James grasps both her hands and holds them tighter and pleads for the chance to find a way to make things right, to fix them, so she can trust him again. He asks her to search with him, and together become who they used to be to one another and find the love they once shared. He talks of the pain and grief of losing Noah and how it was too much for either of them to bear, and how his guilt and sadness took over his life and he stopped noticing her.

'I'm so sorry,' he says, reaching out to hold her.

As the darkness shrouds over the park, Roisin accepts his embrace, and the moment she does so, she feels a wave of relief rush through her body, and they hold on tightly to one another. She didn't know how she was going to move forward with James, or if her hurt and resentment would eventually tear them apart ... All she knew was that she had to try. Roisin then remembers it was in this very park that they first came together as a couple.

'Our tour in France, James, in three weeks' time. I hope it's just the two of us?' Roisin questions.

'Yes,' James replies. 'Yes, yes, just the two of us. I promise you, Roisin, it will always be just the two of us.'

Over the following weeks, when the routine of life resumes, and James has easily put aside his indiscretions, Roisin begins to feel darker, smaller and no longer confident about her future with James; his infidelity has eroded her trust, her once-binding love. She feels no urge for revenge, but James no longer feels like her love and the man she admires, and for her, this is a dangerous state of mind. Time or desperation may force her hand … She may seek out the destructive pleasures, or she may learn to forgive. Roisin believes she will always question whether any man she has loved has ever really known her or put her needs before their own. She thinks not. She is the lost child, the lonely girl, the dreamer of happy beginnings and contented endings. The day after the evening in the park, she played her favourite song by Peter Sarstedt, 'Where Do You Go To My Lovely? She has carried the words of this song with her from the first moment she yearned to be loved, and listening to it brings her solace.

Orla had called her a few days ago; she sounded excited. Annie had signed up on the Ancestry website, having always wanted to know more about her family history, especially the Irish side. Annie feels more Irish than either her mother or aunty ever did.

Roisin remembers Annie telling her years ago that she would listen with her grandfather to his old freedom fighter songs when she was very young. Annie had emailed newspaper cuttings to Roisin: three reports, one from the Maze Prison in Belfast, and the other two from Leicester city courts. Roisin is taken aback at the sight of what she sees on the email. There in black-and-white print is the truth. 'Mr Sean Hugh Quinn was sent down for seven years for planning a bomb attack in the capital on 14 January 1967. He had previously been deported back to Northern Ireland at the age of nineteen for IRA activity.'

A second article in a Leicester newspaper describes the same man as beating and cutting his wife, Anna, and throwing her mother down the stairs. The third article reports on a Mrs Maeve Brennan as serving a four-year sentence for taking a firearm into the Maze Prison in Belfast where her husband Niall was detained and attempting to use the weapon on British soldiers. Roisin sits and reads the articles a few times before ringing Orla.

'At long last,' Roisin says, 'the truth has come out. So that's why dad changed his name to Seamus.' It had nothing to do with hiding from the tax man. She now feels their story is complete.

Three weeks after getting back with James, while in her bedroom and bending down changing an adapter for her phone, Roisin notices a square piece of paper under the bed, perched up against the skirting board. She reaches for it and turns it over ... and to her astonishment there it is, a black-and-white photo of Darra, Orla and herself with their father and his girlfriend Eileen. Their father has his arms around Roisin and her brother's shoulders. Orla's head is snuggled into Eileen's waist. They are all sitting on a stone wall, the rolling waves of the ocean in the background, and golden sand covering their shoeless feet. The children's faces are sun-kissed, smiling and filled with joy, and each child is holding a billowing fluffy cloud of pink candy floss on a stick.

Just as the photo had been hidden in the dark space of the leather suitcase, so had this moment in her life been shut away in the depth of her heart and mind. James walks into the bedroom and sits on the bed next to Roisin. He wraps his arms tightly around her and kisses her tenderly on her forehead. He looks at the photo in her hand and notices a smile come over her.

'That's one I haven't seen before,' he comments.

'So, we did have candy floss on the beach,' Roisin says out loud. 'But why did Darra, Orla and I not remember this moment? Why did we only remember the bad things that happened to us and block out the good? Maybe the memory of pain runs deeper than an act of love.'

She turns and looks at James with tears in her eyes. Noah had every kind of candy floss, but it didn't bring contentment to his troubled mind. If only he had had the time to see how much he was loved. At last, Roisin can see clearly. Her eyes are open wide, her heart is free, she has been fortunate in the most unexpected ways, and she knows she has tasted the real candy floss of life.

ACKNOWLEDGEMENTS

In the beginning, as with most writing, it was just a thought, simmering slowly over time into an undefined theme. Gradually, it began to bubble excitedly into a story, one that made sense to me and filled me with purpose and vision. That vision eventually became a novel: *The Day We Had Candy Floss.*

I would like to express my special thanks of gratitude to all the team at Whitefox Publishing, all of whom gave me the golden opportunity to realise my dream of becoming an author. The completion of this book could not have been accomplished without a 'yes, we are interested,' and the support and steadfast direction from Kiana Palombo, who worked with me at every step, through to publication. I cannot express enough my thanks to Kate Rizzo, the editor whose expertise proved to be exceptional. I would also like to thank Kay Coleman, the copyeditor whose excellent attention to detail weeded out the incompatible, the awkward and the nonsense. She showed me the way to go.

The cover designer, Heike Schüssler, who has captured wonderfully the mystery and sensuality of Roisin. Also, my appreciation goes to Jess King, Marketing Manager at

Whitefox, who has steered the book beyond the office and into your hands, and I am forever grateful to Lucy Mee, for her excellent design, marketing, and social media input.

Also, many thanks go to Seagull Design, who have my eternal gratitude for the quality and care they brought to the layout, ensuring every page reflects the heart of this book. A big shout out to photographer Katie Neeves, for executing a most enjoyable photoshoot, taking me out of my comfort zone, and producing many printed, photogenic versions of myself.

And one can never forget the joy of friends and family, whose interest and advice spurred me on to the finishing line.

Last but not least, I dedicate this book to my husband, David, for being 'the one', and for his love and understanding during my many absences from his company. I also want to acknowledge his often wise suggestions when it came to choosing just the right word or turn of phrase. It has been a passionate journey … one I am keen to replay.

ABOUT THE AUTHOR

As a young girl, Catherine found solace in escape: the poems and stories she wrote in her bedroom became her sanctuary. She dreamed that, given the time and opportunity, she might one day write a novel. After a lifetime on the treadmill of pursuing a career and finding love, her dream came true, and the words effortlessly spilled onto the page. When she is not writing, Catherine can be found at her easel painting, taking long walks with her dogs or somewhere on the ski slopes, waiting for her much-loved husband and friends to show her the way home.

www.ingramcontent.com/pod-product-compliance
Lightning Source LLC
Chambersburg PA
CBHW030254100526
44590CB00012B/397